⚠ WARNING!
READING THIS BOOK
MAY LEAD TO MARRIAGE!

The **Art**

L'Chaim
Publications
TO LIFE!

of the Date

Ruki D. Renov

The ultimate book on finding your perfect match. A complete guide to *shidduch* dating, including instructions, anecdotes, stories, insights and lots of laughs.

ISBN 0-9766946-3-8

Distributed by:
L'Chaim Publications
521 Fifth Avenue
Suite 1740
New York, NY 10175
www.lchaimpublications.com

Cover Illustration: Gadi Pollack
Cover & Book Design: Sruly Perl @ Connections 845.371.2222
Edited by: E. Flam

Printing and Binding by: גל'אור ‖ הוצאה ליאור
Printed in the United States of America

Dedication:

To my loving husband Kal

who is all that I prayed for, and more than I dreamed of.

TABLE OF CONTENTS

INTRODUCTION

In the legendary town of Chelm, two men, quarreling how to determine which of two horses belonged to each of them, went to the town wise man.

"Wise man," said Yankel, "You must help us. We each have a horse and we can't tell which horse is mine and which horse is Shmuli's. How can we tell which horse is which?"

The wise man thought for a moment and then said, "Yankel, you cut the mane on your horse, and Shmuli, you let your horse's mane grow long."

"Oh, brilliant, brilliant," cried the two men.

A few weeks later the two men returned to the wise man. "Please, wisest of men, you must help us. The horses' manes grew back. We can't tell which horse is mine and which horse is his."

The wise man once again thought for a while and said "Yankel, you cut the tail on your horse, and you, Shmuli, let your horse's tail grow long."

"Brilliant, brilliant," cried the two men.

A few weeks later, feeling utterly frustrated, they once again returned to the wise men. "We are desperate," they cried to him. "What should we do? The tails grew back."

The wise man no longer knew what to do. Thinking and thinking, he finally came up with an ingenious idea. "I've got it," cried the wise man, "Yankel, yours is the white horse, and yours Shmuli, is the black horse."

In life, it is always crucial to understand a situation and knowledgably assess the information to make an intelligent decision. Certainly the key to mastering the "*Shidduch* System" is to correctly understand the situation; have a well constructed plan of action; know whom to turn to for advice, whom to trust, how to interpret the information and assess the individuals, and most importantly, how to differentiate and choose the one destined to belong to you.

"It's an impossible situation but it has possibilities."
(Samuel Goldwyn)

Once upon a time matchmaking was easy. G-d created man, formed one of his ribs into a woman, and told them to live together and start building mankind. If only it were that simple today.

The dating system has become a complicated science. The *shidduch* arrangement may have some shortcomings, but also has great benefits; yet it requires instruction, direction and an understanding of the approach, rules and strategies.

This book discusses the strengths and weaknesses of the *shidduch* system, delving into the benefits and drawbacks of research, praising its advantages and criticizing its flaws. It helps you understand what to look for in a spouse and what to over look, what type of person is appropriate for you and what type may be inappropriate. It guides you into finding a *shadchan*, trusting a *shadchan* and becoming a *shadchan* for others.

Some people need the information found in these pages for themselves. Others need it for their sons, daughters, relatives or friends. Although some recommendations are identified as gender-specific, most advice (even if it says "he" or "she") applies to anyone searching for their *"bashert"* (destined partner). The suggestions are also appropriate for parents whose children are dating, since parents are often totally immersed in every aspect of the *shidduch* process.

The questions are never ending: How to meet, whom to meet, where to meet, whom to ask, whom to trust, what to look for, when to date, when to commit and when to walk away are just some examples. The answers are not always simple. In many instances there is no right answer. Often, you need to follow your own instincts and heart.

The initial phone call, the date, and ingredients such as timing, attraction, common goals and interests which propel the couple to get together, enjoy each other's company, stay together or terminate the relationship are analyzed. The proper protocol, meeting the parents, fun dating places versus serious dating places, and what to talk about on a date are some of the topics covered. The engagement, the wedding, support and in-laws are also discussed. The book addresses such topics as where to live (Israel versus U.S.A.), how to treat one another and how to enjoy a long and beautiful relationship.

There are many stories, all of which contain fictional names, in order to assure privacy.

The aim of this book is to guide a person through their search for the right spouse to the fulfillment of a mutually rewarding and wonderful life together.

What a married couple should save for their old age is each other.

The advice in this book is easy to give – unfortunately it is not as easy to follow. Sometimes, I find it hard to execute ideas that I am positive are right. It is hard to let our minds rule our hearts. It is also hard to know when to let our hearts overrule our minds. It is difficult to accept things we don't want to know and difficult to see things we would rather ignore. It can be disturbing to ask questions we know we should ask or to face answers we ourselves don't want to give.

The *shidduch* system is not perfect, but a perfect system has not yet been found. This system does have great potential for success. Therefore, it is smart to be aware of the optimum route and options involved in all aspects of this dating process. Knowing the rules gives you the ability to decide which are appropriate for you and which make you feel most comfortable. Then, you can hopefully make them work in your favor.

Accept advice gracefully - as long as it doesn't interfere with what you intended to do in the first place.

Although this book contains many jokes and humorous anecdotes, it addresses a serious topic and will hopefully give you, the reader, valuable information. It is easier to go through this period with a little humor. I hope this book helps you find temporary laughter and ever-lasting love.

In a seeker's search for wisdom, he spent three painful and grueling weeks climbing a tall rocky mountain. At the peak, he found a wise, old guru

and asked, "Wise man, how might I make my life happier?" The wise man responded, "To begin with, the next time you want to come up here, go to the other side of the mountain and take the lift."

The information in this book will hopefully make the dating process a bit simpler, less stressful, more fun and lead to a joyous and successful marriage.

THE ROAD TO A SHIDDUCH

"Of course life is tough...but what else are we qualified to do?"

What are you in for?

Stress!

There's a story of a man driving along a dark country road, who can't find his way. Finally spying a farmer, he calls out to him, "Do you know how to get to the highway?" "Nope," answers the farmer. "Do you know the way to Route 63?" "Nope," responds the farmer. "Well," asks the driver, "do you know where the nearest gas station is?"

"Nope," is the farmer's reply. "Hey, you don't know much," the driver complains. "True," the farmer says, "but at least I'm not lost."

In the *shidduch* search you can know all the rules and moves, yet still feel helpless and lost. There's no road map, and too many twists, roadblocks and unexpected curves. Just when you think you've mastered the *shidduch* game, the rules seem to change. Nevertheless you must plot a course, and if it doesn't work, readjust, bounce back, and take a new course.

If it's any consolation, everyone feels the same – scared, nervous, overwhelmed, hopeful…You dream and pray. Whether you have everything going for you or not, whether you are "in demand" or have to work hard to find dates, everyone is still nervous – after all, you are choosing someone with whom you will hopefully spend a lifetime.

It is comforting to know we're all in the same boat. So take a deep breath, start rowing, and remember: G-d is at the helm!

Yesterday is experience. Tomorrow is hope. Today is getting from one to the other as best you can.

HASHEM

ೲ⊃C⊆ಀ

"Life is fragile. Handle with prayer."

What has *Hashem* been doing since He created the world? The answer is, of course, He's been making *shidduchim*. It really is a full time job.

For some lucky people a *shidduch* comes easy, but for many this is one of life's tests. One *midrash* says the *nisyonos* we encounter in life, are the ones our *neshamos* asked for before we entered this world. You asked for it - you got it. This period of searching for your or your child's *bashert*, is one of life's tests, a *"nisayon min hashamayim"* (test from Heaven). As with *every nisayon*, we must put in our *hishtadlus* and have *bitachon* in G-d.

"Life is only a test. If it had been the real thing we would have been told where to go and what to do."

We must remember that G-d has a master plan. In each *shidduch* there is a lot of "*Siyatah D'shmayah*". I asked a couple, "Who made your *shidduch*?" They answered, "*Hashem.*" They are so right.

Hashem determines the amount of work a person must do, how many calls he must make, and how many times he must date. Each call you make and each date you go on brings you closer to finding your *bashert*.

It may take time. Perhaps the girl or boy must wait for the other to reach his or her potential. Ultimately, it will be worth the wait.

The Gemara and Chovos Halevovos explain that we don't know who or what is right for our children. So pray for a *shidduch* in a non-specific way, asking *Hashem to* do what's best for your son or daughter.

Everyone knows that making a *shidduch* is as hard as *Kriyas Yam Suf* (splitting the Red Sea). Some nights, while working on a *shidduch* for my kids, I felt I might have been more successful, had I stood at the sink with a knife, trying to cut water. *Kriyas Yam Suf* is going against nature, and in this regard is equivalent to the miraculous combining of two individuals whose lives must mesh into one.

Hashem only performed *Kriyas Yam Suf* once – but He works on *shidduchim* constantly. This should bring a certain sense of comfort to us as we work through this challenging time.

The *Rabbanim* advise us to say *Tehillim*, turning our hearts to G-d, because only *Hashem* can really make *shidduchim*. Our job is to put in our *hishtadlus* and then say, "*Hashem*, I'm doing my *hishtadlus*, please do Yours." Remember that everything is in G-d's hands. Every match is *Min Hashamayim* – Heaven made. So *daven*, do *chessed*, and put in as much effort as you can. Say *Shir Hashirim* and have *bitachon*.

A man went to heaven. There he met G-d who showed him the footprints of his life. Looking, the man saw that in most places there were two sets of footprints, his and G-d's, but in a few spots there were only one set of prints. The man said to G-d, "I don't understand. I thought you promised me that you would always walk with me. Why do I see only one set of footprints at times?" "Those", answered G-d, "were the times that I carried you."

This is a difficult period when *Hashem* must carry, guide and bless each of us, but we must do our part. Here is how you begin:

GETTING STARTED

I am reminded of a young lad who rushed breathlessly to the train platform just as the last car pulled away. A man standing nearby, observing the incident, smiled sympathetically at the boy. "I guess you did not run fast enough." "Oh, yes, I did," the boy responded. "I just didn't start soon enough."

The beginning is the hardest with most projects, but dating, like childbirth, may be difficult from start to finish. People have told me that marrying off their children was like opening a jar of pickles. The first one is hard to extract, but after that the others pop out easily. I haven't found this to be true. Each child presents a new experience and challenge.

Parents should get ready to gain or lose weight, stay up nights and consider taking Valium. But then take control of yourself, decide never to get discouraged, and begin.

For the young woman or man who is just starting the dating process, this can be a wonderful and exciting time of life. Enjoy the experience. Delight in meeting different people. Learn to become comfortable with men or women and gain experience at getting to know what you are looking for, and with whom you enjoy spending time.

Girls should start early because the competition is enormous. A common complaint is "for a boy you need a secretary whereas for a girl you need a press agent." Unfortunately, girls always feel the time pressure, whereas boys think, "If I don't find someone now, I'll wait for the next crop."

There seems to be less pressure searching for dates for boys, because they have the advantage of being inundated with suggestions. They get to choose first and they don't have to care about age. However, believe it or not, feeling overwhelmed by so many suggestions, can turn this into a disadvantage. Someone told me it will be my turn to be in the driver's seat when my son dates. They failed to mention that I would be driving twenty hours a day – researching, researching, and researching. Remember too, that even after names are suggested, it is not simple to get both sets of parents as well as the boy and girl to agree to the date and be available at the same time.

Mrs. Cohen told me her daughter had just returned from Israel and wanted to start dating, but she thought her daughter should wait. I lectured Mrs. Cohen about how fast time flies, telling her not to wait because the good boys are snatched up quickly. I added that she must get to work, spreading the word about her daughter and researching possibilities. When Mrs. Cohen told me she had just taken a job because she didn't have what to do, I jokingly replied, "Give up the job, now you have work to do." In a matter of moments I turned a calm, happy woman into a worried nervous wreck. "Where do I start? What do I do? Whom do you know?" etc. Reality hurts but I truly felt I was doing her a favor. It's smart to be aware of how hard the *shidduch* process can be and work on it as early as possible.

Anyone who starts dating should be ready and mature enough to get married. In general, girls are ready sooner, but it really depends on the individual. Most girls are ready between the ages of nineteen and twenty-one, while boys usually feel ready between the ages of twenty and twenty-four, but there are always exceptions. Each child, together with his or her parents must decide when he or she is ready for *tachlis* and determine when it is appropriate to start dating.

It isn't easy being single these days. I have a mother who wants me to eat and a doctor who wants me to diet.

Look the best you can – watch your weight and buy flattering clothing. Girls should wear the right makeup. Boys should look neat and well groomed. Now is the time to care. Now is when it counts.

"Unless you have sent one out, it's no use waiting for your ship to come in."

Spread the word. The person beginning to date and/or the parents must inform everyone that you or your child is ready to start going out. Call rabbis, principals, old and new friends, relatives, neighbors, and *shadchanim*. Don't be embarrassed to ask if they know of anyone and to keep you, your daughter or son in mind. Talk to everyone and anyone – you never know who has a son, daughter, nephew, friend, etc. Every time you ask someone for a suggestion and they mention a name, you are one idea richer.

Get exposure – go to weddings, major events, conventions, fund raisers, Bar-Mitzvahs, weekends, *shul* and school events. Let people know you or your child are going out or, as it is commonly referred to, "has entered the *parshah*".

Parents, in particular, should talk to everyone. It is a parent's responsibility to let everyone know the good news – your child is ready, and the right person will be very lucky to have him or her as their *zivug*.

Take the best picture you can and ask your family members to carry it around, showing it when appropriate. Take along a small camera to various events, so you or your parents can snap a photo of someone who interests you, helping you find out who the person is. People are usually flattered if someone takes a picture of them, however camera phones make this part of the job quite inconspicuous.

I once complained that I am constantly trying to see who is available. An engaged or married girl usually wears a ring or a *sheitel*. But how can I tell if a boy is single?

"Look at his wrist," someone advised. In religious circles, if he is wearing a fancy watch, he is usually "taken", wearing the watch given to him by his in-laws. Of course, the watch is usually covered by the boy's cuff, so now, wherever I go, I ask the boys for the time; they must pull up their cuffs to see the time and I can check out their wristwatches.

Speak to people and collect names, keeping a notebook. This notebook will prove to be valuable, so much so, that I've heard of people who sold their book of names of available boys or girls.

The notebook should have the names of boys or girls who have been suggested to you, or whom you have heard of and would like to meet. Alongside each name write who suggested the person and who can *rhed* (arrange) the *shidduch*. Then list everything you've heard about this person, making sure to include who said it so you can judge how reliable a source it is. It should include the person's *Shidduchagram* (see next paragraph). This notebook is also the place to keep track of whom you dated, how often you dated them, and what you thought of them. Not only will this clarify your thoughts, it also helps if at some later date you want to reconsider this person. This notebook can also useful to help others who are going through this.

Prepare what I call a *"Shidduchagram"* (sample below), which lists all your personal information and answers to the most commonly asked questions. This should resemble a resume.

Carrying a paper listing all relevant information will make you seem efficient rather than desperate. You can say you printed this up because thank G-d so many people have asked about you, your son or your daughter. You can also say you wrote this up to make it easier for people, "since these days, you know how it is, everyone asks so many questions."

If enough people do it, eventually a *Shidduchagram* will become the trend, and just as people ask each other for business cards or work resumes, they will say, "Do you have your *Shidduchagram*, bio or personal resume?" when you mention yourself, your son or daughter.

An expert knows all the answers - if you ask the right questions.

SAMPLE SHIDDUCHAGRAM:

- Name
- Age
- Phone, cell, fax, email or web page
- Address
- Parents' names
- Parents' occupations
- *Shul*
- Family affiliations
- School – *Yeshiva*, high school, college, Israel – (This usually categorizes the person.)
- Camp
- Other organizations
- *Yichus* (heritage)
- Grandparents

- Siblings
- Other *mechutanim* (sibling's in-laws) of your parents
- Type of family i.e. open house, involved, close, warm, private, charitable
- Religious status i.e. *Kovaya Itim* (scheduled learning), *Rebbe, Baal Teshuva,* Black hat, *Yeshivish,* modern, growing.
- Personality i.e. quiet, outgoing, reserved, sweet upbeat, kind, good-natured
- Personal characteristics i.e. pretty, handsome, tall, short, bright, pleasant looking.
- Type you're looking for i.e. capable, great family, fine, fun loving, *baal chessed,* warm, loving, talented, athletic, personable, enjoys learning, good singer, color war captain, well rounded.
- Dreams i.e. open to living in Israel, love lots of children
- Future plans i.e. learning, *kollel, chinuch,* medical school, business, working or any combination – also known as "learner-earner, or earner-learner?"
- Height
- References i.e. names, position, phone number
- You may include a picture.

List the character traits you are looking for in a person in your "Wish List". Try to be specific about what you are looking for, but be flexible about whom you agree to date. Don't limit yourself too much – give leeway. It is hard to know what you are looking for until you find it. People often surprise themselves with whom they marry. (See chapter "You Never Know.")

Though most people fix you up with whomever they know, rather than with someone who meets your description of what you are looking for, it is still worth trying to give some direction and guidelines.

Your list of references should consist of people who know you or your family, who are able to give a good and thorough recommendation. Have your local Rabbi get to know you and your parents so he can serve as a reference. Get close to teachers, principals, *Yeshiva* and important community members so they can tell others what you are like.

This type of resume will save you being asked lots of questions and will give the *shadchanim* lots of answers at their fingertips. Put thought into your answers, because just as a business resume determines if you land an interview, the *Shidduchagram* can determine whether you get a date. Use this form as a guide, not a Bible, adding to or modifying it to make it work for you. Deleting certain information or leaving out a picture is quite all right. Not including a photo does not necessarily mean the person isn't good looking. It may mean the person is modest or doesn't have a picture with which she or he is happy.

Just about the time we finally learn all the answers, they change the questions.

Decide where you will most likely find the type of person you are looking for, by determining which school or *yeshiva* produces the boy or girl you want. Find out who the *Rav*, the principal, the *Mashgiach* (overseer) or the dorm counselor in the *yeshiva* is, and have someone call him - or be brave and call him yourself. Be prepared to tell him what you are looking for, what you are like and whom he can call to verify what you are telling him. A woman can call a *Rosh Yeshiva* to ask for a *shidduch,* or to ask about a boy, questioning whether a *shidduch* seems appropriate.

In many circles parents are in control of the entire process and then of course it is appropriate for them to make these calls. In other cases the boy or girl "in the parshah" are the ones involved in placing the calls.

It is important that you give a principal or *Rosh Yeshiva* reliable references, when you ask him to help you or your child find someone, especially if the *Rav* is not familiar with you.

Contact the best *shadchan* for you (discussed in chapter "The Shadchan").

Ask your friends to fix you up with people who may not be for them. As Avi was ending a relationship with a girl, he spotted his friend Simon in the same hotel lobby with another girl. Immediately Avi thought that Simon would be perfect for the girl with whom he was breaking up, and after the date Avi called Simon to set him up with her. Simon married her.

Ask your newly engaged friends who their intended's friends are, names of other people they dated, and who else was on their list of possible *shidduchim*.

One novel but helpful idea is for the friends of a newly engaged couple to wear name tags to the *vort*. This would be a casual way for singles or their parents to check out those still available. Though some people may cringe at this when they're younger, often they are more nervous and therefore willing to do things to help themselves by the time they turn twenty-one. If we institute these types of ideas, making them acceptable and considered the norm, it can make the meeting and *shidduch* process more effective.

Fix up your friends – they'll do the same for you. My good friend Marilyn was set up with Eli from Chicago; though Marilyn felt he was not for her, she thought he was perfect for her best friend Sandy. She arranged for Sandy and Eli to meet. They got married. Sandy moved to Chicago and fixed Marilyn up with Eli's best friend Sam whom she married. Marilyn too moved to Chicago. Together, Marilyn and Sandy fixed up their third out of town girl friend with Sam and Eli's other best friend and miraculously, this too worked out. All three girl friends live near one another in Chicago and are always arranging *shidduchim* for people.

Put aside plenty of time for phone calls - either to ask people for suggestions or to research those persons already mentioned. You also need to make phone calls to search for the best person to arrange the *shidduch* and push for the date.

When my kids are in this phase of their lives, I work for hours making contacts and checking out leads. It's a full time job. I am busy until 11 p.m. making calls in New York, and then I start calling Chicago and the Midwest area since they are an hour behind. California contacts are next because I have an extra three hours of calling time. Finally, I call friends and suggested contacts in Israel. By the time I finish those calls, I'm lucky to get a few hours of sleep before the cycle begins again.

Even if a girl or boy has many names suggested to him/her, it does not mean the offer is solid. It's a long and often discouraging process from hearing the suggestion to making the date happen. Mrs. Laub, informing me that she had been told about four great men for her daughter, asked me to check into them. One boy was not yet dating, one was already seeing someone else, and the third had a long list of names he was checking. The last one only wanted a girl who had gone to a particular seminary. Though Mrs. Laub's daughter had gone to a terrific seminary, it was not the one on this boy's required list. So even though Mrs. Laub thought she had four potential prospects for her daughter, in reality, she was at square one.

You have to get on the other person's "list". Try to find the best connections and people to recommend you, so you are moved to the top of the list of the person you want to date.

After finding someone you would like to ask out, or someone you would like to have ask you out, both of your schedules need to jive. A boy may already have committed to taking someone else out first, even if he wants to date this girl. So too, a girl may have agreed to date someone else first, though she agrees to date this boy. Both individuals have to be available at the same time. You or the *shadchan* must stay on top of the situation until the timing works out for both the girl and boy involved. This often gets quite complex and is one of the most frustrating parts of the *shidduch* system.

Look in your own circles. Consider your parents' friends' children, the *Rebbe* who teaches at your brother's school, the tutor in your home or people who are active in your *shul* or school. Consider your sisters' or brothers' friends. My ten year old daughter often comes home from school telling me to look into her teacher or substitute who she believes may be right for my son. It is amazing at how early you can make people aware that fixing others up is important and a wonderful *mitzvah*.

A mother of a single Jewish girl was driving home from work one evening when she saw a man trying to hitch a ride. She picked him up and they began talking.

"What do you do?" she asked him.

"I recently escaped from prison where I was serving a life sentence for killing my wife."

"Oh, does that mean you're available?"

One grandmother told her daughter, Mrs. Fine, to fix up her granddaughter Sara. Sara's brother Yoni had terrific friends who often joined the family at the *Shabbos* table. The Grandmother continually urged her daughter to choose one of Yoni's friends for Sara and "tie him to the leg of the table." However, Mrs. Fine, concentrating on fixing up her son Yoni since he was two years older, told her mother to stop worrying. Then one of Yoni's friends, a frequent visitor at the Fine *Shabbos* table, got engaged. Mrs. Fine was devastated. She had let this wonderful young man, whom she knew and was comfortable with, slip right through her fingers.

Besides looking and asking around, consider the following suggestions:

Check out the Internet. Of course, you must exercise caution, making sure the site is reliable and respectable. I know quite a few people who met this way. If you type in Jewish Dating on your search engine, many options appear; some of these offer free membership while others have a low monthly or yearly fee. It is worth a try. FutureSimchas.com is now up and running. SawYouAtSinai. com. has over two hundred *shadchanim* on line to help Orthodox singles. You must decide which website works for you. JDate.com, for example, has over 300,000 singles registered but this includes Reform and Conservative as well as Orthodox Jews. Frumsters specializes in Orthodox Jews. There are many sites with bios, pictures and referrals.

Attend events and weekends sponsored and endorsed by respectable *Yeshivos*. (See chapter "*Shidduch* System Versus Meet on Your Own".)

Attend or have your name brought up at *shidduch* meetings. (See chapter "The *Shadchan*")

Speed dating through an organization called *Aish Hatorah* has become a successful way to meet new people.

For those who accept meeting in a social setting, papers like The Jewish Press often list singles events.

Encourage people to fix you up with someone. Be persistent. "The wheel that squeaks loudest is most oiled." You have the right to keep reminding people to fix you up, because they unintentionally forget.

Ask friends, network, decide whom you will agree to date, and get on peoples' lists.

Obstacles are those frightening things you see when you take your eyes off the goal.

The thing to try when all else fails is "again". Keep at it. Don't get discouraged.

Take on a new *mitzvah*. Rabbis have advised that saying *Tehillim* (Psalm 19) and practicing *Shmiras Halashon* are helpful in bringing favorable results to the *shidduch* arena.

Before you start dating, it is important to be tested for genetically carried diseases such as Tay Sachs, Cystic Fibrosis and others. This simple blood test which helps determine genetic compatibility is done by *DOR YESHORIM* (718-384-6060). The results of the test are kept confidential even from the person being tested. After being tested, before you date someone, call *DOR YESHORIM* and inform them of your prospective *shidduch*; if that person has also been tested, they can tell you whether or not you are compatible. This can save a lot of heartache later on.

To summarize: Get exposure, circulate your personal bio or *Shidduchagram*, determine what you are looking for, get names, improve your good deeds, get tested, and get to work by starting your research.

"She's a lovely person. She deserves a good husband. Marry her before she finds one." *(Marx Brothers)*

RESEARCH
ℯℯ◯Ⲥℯℯ

In making my decision, I must admit that I have allowed facts to influence my thinking.

It took Alexander Graham Bell twenty years to invent the telephone. It took his wife one minute to invent the busy signal! It takes me days and nights of research to find a boy worthy of going out with my daughter, and then, within three minutes of meeting the young man, my daughter can judge him favorably or reject him.

My grandfather used to say, "A boy and a girl is a *glacha* (perfect) *shidduch*." He was right. But a girl wants more than just any boy, and a boy wants more than just any girl.

Research, the most fundamental aspect of the *shidduch* system, is vital. It is an initial screening process that helps narrow the field of available prospects. Finding out all you can about the person and his family, discovering his character, ideals, values, goals and expectations, ascertaining his strengths and even becoming familiar with his imperfections, helps you determine whether this person might be right for you. Research, if done correctly by asking the right questions to reliable and trustworthy individuals, is invaluable and highly advisable.

What's right for one person is not necessarily right for some one else. Once in Loehman's, I followed a well-dressed woman around to see what she was buying. I watched her try on a gorgeous coat, and when she put it down, I grabbed it. I didn't care that it wasn't my size and that it was made for a woman twice my height. The coat looked ridiculous on me and it sat in my closet, unworn and good for nothing. The same is true with a *shidduch*. Sometimes you grab a certain boy or girl only because you hear someone else wants him, but that doesn't mean he or she is for you. A boy or girl is also worthless if he is wrong for you, although he may be great for someone else.

What's the difference between a blind date and a *shidduch* date? One usually goes into a blind date eyes closed, knowing very little about the person. But, you are usually totally enlightened on a *shidduch* date, having found out as much as you can about your date. The key to *shidduch* dating is to do your RESEARCH.

The *Chofetz Chaim* said that before a prospective couple meet, certain criteria regarding background, level of observance, family and future intentions must be met. These objectives, including financial obligations, should be agreed on before the couple invests emotional involvement by meeting each other.

Some people have a thick book of names, but no dates. They collect names and keep researching, but either they can't choose anyone they want to date, or can't find anyone to agree to date them.

Other people, known as "serial daters", date everyone they hear of without doing any research, never stopping until they meet the right one.

Once a name is suggested to you or you hear of someone that interests you, you must find out if he has begun dating. There are many levels to consider. They include:

• He is thinking of starting to date.

• He is going to start to date.

• He may be able to be convinced to start to date.

• He is starting to date but he's not taking names yet.

• He is starting to date after Succoth, Pesach or the summer.

• He'll take the name but is not promising anything.

• He is dating but he has too many names right now.

• The boy is not ready.

• The boy is "in the middle of a *Parshah*" in other words, he's seeing someone now.

• He's "busy".

• The boy just "started a new *Parshah*".

The boy won't date the girl until six months after her return from Israel. (Some boys wait to see if the girls "normalize"- in other words, temper some of their idealism and come down to reality, after the intense Israel experience. Similarly, some girls don't want to date boys until six months after their return from Israel, to make sure the boys maintain their high level of seriousness and dedication to learning.)

The boy is "in the freezer" but when he "defrosts he's going to melt fast". He'll put the girl on his "list". (Lakewood boys can't date for the first three months after they have started learning at the *Yeshiva,* unless they had started dating the girl before beginning *Yeshiva*)

The suggested match doesn't sound "*shayach*" (relevant).

He'll get back to you. Don't call him – he'll call you.

He or his parents will "research" the suggested girl and get back to you.

Smart people never say outright that they are not interested. It is never worth hurting people's feelings.

A nineteen-year old boy is usually too young to date, but you'd better ask if he's starting to date when he is twenty years old. Usually he's not, but he might start soon. In the *Chassidish* world boys do get married at eighteen.

Many people don't admit they are dating, and then they are suddenly engaged. Some people never even come "on the market". If you are interested in a certain boy or girl, keep track, asking about and researching him or her. Make sure your name gets to him or to her as soon and as often as possible (without overdoing it).

A boy or girl, unsure whether to date or not, often feels ready to get married after the first dating experience. Even if the first person you date was not right for you, it awakens the urge to meet the right one.

When you research a person, every one sounds the same. Everyone tells you he's "a great boy"; she's "a terrific girl". It seems that everyone comes from a lovely family and is really nice looking, very bright, etc. Every description sounds wonderful, but only some individuals really are, and even if they are all terrific, they are certainly all different. Each person has qualities that will or will not appeal to you. Make sure to ask the right people and get truthful answers.

There are appropriate and relevant questions to ask when one is researching someone, including those discussed in the *Shidduchagram* (see chapter "Getting Started").

"A fool can ask more questions than a wise man can answer."

Unfortunately, people have gotten carried away with research and ask some ridiculous questions today. Though everyone admits they have gotten out of hand, many people seem pulled into asking these superficial questions. It is vital for people to look inside a person, into his/her essence, asking appropriate questions.

The following is a sample of the inconsequential questions people now ask about the girl or boy and their families:

• Do they use a white tablecloth on *Shabbos*?

• Do they use plastic tablecloths?

• Does the mother place a ketchup, mustard or horseradish jar directly on the *Shabbos* table, as opposed to putting the condiment in a fancy dish?

• Does the mother wear sneakers in the street?

• Does the mother or grandmother use a shopping cart to walk through the street?

• Does the boy wear his hat to take out the garbage?

• Does he wear shoes with laces? (Slip-on shoes are thought to be a sign of laziness, not of preference or comfort.)

• Does the girl wear patent leather shoes?

• Does the girl chew gum?

• What does the father wear when he plays tennis? If he doesn't play tennis – what would he wear if he did play tennis?

• What type of orange juice do they drink? (Tropicana is not considered *heimish* even though it has an OU. And is delicious)

• Do they use cloth or paper napkins at the *Shabbos* table?

• Does the girl wear nail polish? If so, what color?

• Does the girl wear a seat belt on a date? (This may accentuate the girl's figure, and ridiculously some people reject a girl who wants to wear a seat belt. I believe in safety first. There's a story of a girl who got stuck on a ski lift with a boy, and to avoid being alone with him, she jumped off and broke her leg. Judge this one for yourself.

• Is she "GU" – geographically undesirable? (Many men don't want to travel too far to pick up a date.)

•Is she a "sushi girl"? (Try to figure that one out.)

•Is she a JAP (Jewish American Princess)? Some people may not want a girl who is high maintenance. The answer to this question is always very subjective.

What does a JAP make for dinner? Reservations.

There are questions that help categorize a person. Some are important although you really can't judge a person based solely on these answers. Every individual is unique. These questions include:

Do they have a TV in the house? This question is relevant, but people often say they don't have one even if they do have a TV. Perhaps they consider a TV hidden behind a cabinet door as not having one. Even if people have three TVs behind doors they often say they don't have any. One should also take into account the reason why a person does or does not possess a TV. Is it for a religious or an intellectual reason?

Does the boy or girl see movies? This too is relevant because it reflects a life style and a *hashkafah*, yet this answer is also usually unclear. Some people go to movie theaters, while others don't go to theatres but do rent movies. Some people watch movies only on their computers. Still others watch rented movies but don't go into Blockbuster or Hollywood Video themselves; rather someone else rents the movies for them. (If you watch movies but don't rent movies, it is smart to marry someone who does rent movies even if he won't watch movies.) All these people might say they don't see movies. Everyone has their moral or religious reason why they do or don't do whatever it is they do and that's okay. But if the question matters to you, find out the real answer. Deciding whether to meet someone should not depend on whether he watches movies he rents or watches movies someone brings home. Also, even if a girl or boy does watch TV or movies, perhaps they would be willing to give this up for the right person.

Do they allow newspapers in the house?

Do you hold by the *Eruv*? (This gives you the option of carrying things on the Sabbath) A girl waited a year for a boy to return from Israel to date her. He called and asked, "Do you hold by the *Eruv*"? She said, "Yes." He said, "I can't go out with you," without even discussing the issue. Perhaps had he made her understand his reasons for not holding by the *Eruv*, she would have agreed with him.

Other questions that help categorize a person are:

• Will the girl cover her hair? How much? Including bangs?

• Will the girl wear a *sheitel*, a fall or only snoods?

• Will the girl shave her head?

• Does the boy wear a black hat? All the time or only on *Shabbos*?

• Does the boy wear colored or striped shirts?

• Does the boy wear a black velvet *yarmulka* or a *kippa seruga* (knitted *yarmulka*)? What size?

• Does the boy have a beard or *payos* (religious side burns)?

• Does the girl belong to N.C.S.Y. (National Council of Synagogue Youth)?

• Does the girl always wear socks?

• Does the boy or girl's mother cover her hair?

• Does the boy or girl's mother wear pants?

• Does the boy or girl's father learn or set aside regular time for Torah study?

In my opinion, questions worth asking also include:

• What is the person's *hashkafah*?

• What is the family's reputation?

• What is the person's schooling?

• Which camps did the person attend?

• Will the boy work? If so, at what?

• What type of learner is the boy?

• How many hours a day will the boy learn?

• For how many years will the boy learn?

• What type of student is he?

• Will the girl work? If so, at what?

• Does the girl or boy do Chesed work such as working with cancer patients, or volunteering in a hospital, or working with special children? Of course, people change with the circumstances of life and no answer is etched in stone.

• Who are his good friends? His teachers? His *Yeshiva*?

• Where does he or she hope to live? Where is he or she willing to live?

• Will the family help financially?

• Is there any major illness that runs in the family?

Include all questions listed in the *Shidduchagram*. (See chapter "Getting Started".)

First woman: "What do you mean by telling your boyfriend that I was deaf and dumb?"
Second woman: "I didn't say deaf."

I have heard stories where no research was done, either because a person's suggestion was just followed or because someone pressured the person about an available girl or boy without allowing him time to check into the proposed *shidduch*. In some of these cases the *shidduchim* worked out, and in others they were a total failure. Of course, this can happen even when considerable research is done. Sometimes the couple like each other but the parents are unhappy, sorry they didn't check out the girl or boy before the relationship progressed. Therefore a rule of thumb is to do whatever research you can without overdoing it. Be sure of the source and accuracy of your research. Furthermore, be careful how you interpret and judge the importance of the things you hear about a person. If the person seems to fit your main qualifications, meet him. Remember, "A picture is worth a thousand words." Meeting someone for yourself is often worth more than or certainly as much as the research.

Sam asked his friend Irv, why he was still single at the age of forty. Irv said, "Every time my mother researches the girl I'm interested in, she dislikes her." Sam said, "Find a girl who is just like your mother, then your mother will have to approve of her." Irv thought this was a great idea. A year later, Sam and Irv met again. Sam asked, "Did you take my advice. Did you find a woman who is just like your mother?" "Yes," answered Irv. "Did your mother like her?" "Yes, my mother met her and checked her out and she loved her." "So," asked Sam, "did you marry her?" "No," said Irv. "Why not?" Sam questioned. "Because," said Irv, "my father hated her."

PROBLEMS WITH RESEARCH

There is so much research to do in the *shidduch* system that my children tell people their mother's occupation is "Research Analyst" at this point.

A person must add up to 100%, but percentages can be distributed in different ways. You may care about finding someone with looks, brains, family, sweetness, wealth, charisma, talent, personality, a career, a good education, a good learner and a potential for growth. You may wind up marrying someone where the distribution or proportion of these characteristics is different than what you had hoped for, but you won't feel you are settling because you know the total person. However, when the name is being researched and you hear s/he is only mediocre looking, you may reject the person, though had you met him/her, you might have been attracted by his or her intelligence and personality.

What if you find out that the person you are researching is balding, heavy, or a drop too tall or too short? Even if everything else about that person is perfect, unfortunately, you might not give him/her a chance. You have to look at the whole person. Meet the person and judge for yourself.

When someone, researching a particular individual, asks you questions, how honest an answer should you give? It's a delicate balance. Even though many leading Rabbinic authorities believe you are allowed to speak *Lashon Hara* when it is pertinent to the *shidduch*, people still tend to lie or omit mentioning things they know may hurt the *shidduch*. People are nervous their comments may get back to the people they are speaking of, and sadly, this is often the case. Despite this fear, it is vital not to withhold necessary information for safety reasons or the like. People also tend to omit vital information if they feel the person asking really needs a *shidduch*. It is not your place to omit something you know. Tell the facts and allow the person to make an informed decision.

People also tend to inject their own feelings into the mix of information, which can be another problem. Someone focused on looks, may feel a boy is not good looking enough for a particular girl, but the girl may not care about looks as much. A good learner or a great personality can make up for his appearance.

Listen with a grain of salt when other people say things like, "He's too quiet for you" or "She's not pretty enough for you." Don't be completely persuaded when people say, "Trust me. He's not for you." You yourself don't really know who and what will appeal to you; someone else certainly can't know. (See chapter "You Never Know".)

Intuition is a case of mind over data.

Just because a person says, "Trust me," doesn't mean you have to. If your research convinces you that someone may be for you, don't worry about hurting the feelings of a person you asked who says s/he is not for you. Handle it wisely by saying, "Please don't be upset. I value your opinion, but there are certain things I heard about this girl that make me want to meet her and see for myself."

People suggesting a *shidduch* may be upset if you don't give them the courtesy of a response. Though it may be difficult finding time to respond to each suggestion, it is nice to try. Of course, we hope people understand there are not enough hours to research everyone or get back to everyone. Furthermore, some people may be offended, feeling you don't trust their taste when you are not interested in their suggestion. People say, "what's the big deal – it's just one date." It's not – it's time and energy. It's time lost from dating others, it's frustrating and tiring, and can become costly for the boy.

Finding out which other people someone may have dated is not necessarily reliable research. People often say, "If he dated her, it's not for me." That's not true. After you meet Mr. or Mrs. Right, you often discover that s/he dated some of your closest friends, as well as others who are totally different from you.

When you feel someone's suggestion is not appropriate, the less said the better. Say, "Right now my son or daughter is busy." Or "We'll keep the name in mind but presently we are looking into some others." If you detail why you don't want the *shidduch*, people can say you didn't give it a chance. You're accused of being superficial if you use looks, weight, or height, as reasons to say no to a *shidduch*. (see chapter "Appearances - Attraction".)

When you reject someone's suggestion people often take it personally. Even the *shadchan* may bring his or her issues and hang-ups into the picture. A *shadchan*, trying to fix up Michael, was told by his mother that she heard the girl wasn't pretty. The *shadchan,* upset, said she couldn't believe how superficial this mother and son were. The mother realized the *shadchan* wasn't very pretty, and may have had a hard time being fixed up herself. Though another *shadchan* may have said, "Fine. Michael cares about looks so this girl is not for him," this *shadchan* brought her own issues to the mix.

A wife had her face lifted, her nose straightened, her stomach tucked, her eyes shaped, and then she turned to her husband and said, "You're not the same man I married!"

You must give people a chance but neither do you want to waste yours or the other person's time. If you know your son is turned off by a heavy, short, or very tall girl, but you heard that she's fabulous, try to convince him to go out despite the height or weight. But if he feels he's never attracted to this type of girl, why waste both their time and energy? And if the *shadchan* is heavy, very short or very tall and can't relate to your reason for not accepting the *shidduch*, don't justify or defend your son's feelings. Everyone has a right to his feelings.

It is difficult not to offend people. Your child may refuse to go out with your friend's child. This sensitive issue must be handled delicately. People use excuses such as, "It is better if they don't date just in case it doesn't work out" or "I would love for them to date but my son feels our families are too close…" Do your best to be sincere yet evasive and hope your friend realizes you or your child doesn't feel the match will work. Do not give a reason that sounds silly or unrealistic. A friend of mine once said her son couldn't date another woman's daughter because her daughter was "too perfect." How do you argue with that excuse?

The trouble with advice is you can't tell if it's good or bad until you've taken it.

Josh introduced a girl he was dating to his friend. Later, he asked the friend what he thought of her. The friend said Josh could do better. That night Josh announced his engagement to that same girl. His friend was horrified. He had truly thought Josh wanted his opinion. This friend said he would never again give an opinion.

Honesty has one great advantage. You never have to remember anything!

Often you are just as busy researching the *shadchan* or person you are questioning, as you are researching the boy or girl you are looking into, since both need to be researched. If a *shadchan* is reliable with a good reputation, you are more comfortable with the information he is giving you. A *shadchan*, or the person you are questioning, may have personal reasons for skewing his information and saying positive things about the boy or girl. He may be related to the boy or girl, perhaps he is thinking of the money or appreciation he hopes to receive, or possibly he is overly excited about making a *shidduch*. On the other hand, a *shadchan* or the person being questioned may have personal reasons for discouraging the *shidduch*. He may have a relative of his own that he wants you or the boy/girl you are asking about to date. Or, he may have a personal issue with the girl/boy you are researching.

Be cautious about the people you enlist to help you with your research. It may be hard to ask friends about other people, especially if they themselves are in the *parshah*. Either she may be interested in the boy, or while researching him for you, she may find that his profile matches what she is searching for, making it difficult for her to set him up with you. My grandmother used to say, "Don't send a cat to get milk."

At times, even your best friends may be envious. If your friend wants her daughter to date your son, she may be insulted if you ask her what she thinks about another girl for your son. It's a delicate issue.

Don't look at the messenger, look at the message. You may not love the person suggesting the *shidduch*,but he may be suggesting someone terrific.

Be smart and research a person quietly. Only ask those who you feel can really be objective and helpful.

It is always worth listening to close relatives who have your interest at heart. Although you may not always agree with them, you can always trust their good intentions.

If the rule, as I have been told, is "Don't ask a friend, don't tell a friend," then whom do you ask?

Can you trust the Rabbi? Most Rabbis are an excellent choice to turn to for a reference. Most *Roshei Yeshivos* are aware of the *halachos* pertaining to *shidduchim*. A good many of them are experienced in dealing with social and marital issues. Their objectives are generally sincere and well meaning. If you have a relationship with a Rabbi, you can trust him to be honest about the boy or girl. But a problem may arise if the boy or girl or his or her family is also close with this Rabbi. The Rabbi must be very careful about what he says.

If the Rabbi you are questioning is the Rabbi of the boy or girl you are researching, his loyalty must be to his congregant. Though he won't lie, he may not reveal everything he knows if it is detrimental to the boy, the girl or either of their family's character. Sara called Joseph's Rabbi, and asked him to tell her all about her fiancé to be, before getting engaged. The Rabbi omitted mentioning that Joseph was divorced and had a child. Sara called off the engagement when she found out about it later, feeling there was no honesty in the relationship. When she confronted Joseph's Rabbi, asking why he hadn't mentioned these facts, the Rabbi said Joseph and his family were good members of his *shul* and he did not want to ruin a *shidduch*. Joseph should have told Sara, but the Rabbi, aware that he hadn't, should have revealed the information to Sara, perhaps explaining that Joseph was scared to tell her for fear of losing her. Since Sara was calling the Rabbi in good faith to find out what he knew of her fiancé, the Rabbi was obligated to tell her.

After checking with a *Rosh Yeshiva*, and hearing only good things about him, one man allowed his daughter to marry a certain boy. Sadly, it turned out that the boy was disturbed; the *Rosh Yeshiva* had suspected it but hadn't mentioned it to the girl's father. When the father asked him why he hadn't mentioned it, the *Rosh Yeshiva* said though he had heard there was an incident with this boy, he was hoping a good girl would solve his problem. Unfortunately, the *Rosh Yeshiva*, with the best of intentions, had taken a chance with someone else's life.

The *Rabbanim* have *paskened* (ruled) that one can not lie about anything that could be relevant to a *shidduch* (*midvar sheker tirchak-*distance yourself from lies). Included in this category of facts to be revealed are physical, psychological and psychiatric conditions that interfere with the person's ability to function as a spouse or parent, as well as any serious condition in the family that is hereditary. This information need not be revealed at an initial meeting so the person does have a chance, but must be revealed before any emotional attachment is developed.

Most often people don't lie; rather they hurt you by omission. I heard someone asking about a boy. She was smart enough to tell the person she was questioning, "Don't '*dray me a kup*' (spin my head) – tell it to me straight."

My friend was asked about Karen. Though she disliked Karen's mother, she didn't want to say anything bad, but neither did she feel capable of saying anything good. She therefore told the caller she didn't know the family well and suggested they contact Karen's mother's closest friend. This may seem decent, but only hearing about the family from someone who likes them without hearing why someone else disapproves of them gives the caller a distorted view of what Karen's family is like. This is doing the researcher, who is looking for a reliable source, a major disservice. The proper behavior would have been for my friend to say, "I don't get along with Karen's mother for these reasons, but call her friend to get a more balanced picture."

Some people feel, "Why bother researching? People only say nice things - great boy, nice family." I have heard horrifying and heart breaking stories of girls who married boys (even from good families) who beat or molested their wives. Did people who were asked purposely not tell what the boy was like? Did they not know?

Did they suspect but not say? Did they feel it wasn't their place to voice their suspicions or opinions? Did they feel a loyalty to the boy's family? Did they fear it would get back to the boy's family had they bad-mouthed him? Did they hope someone else would tell the girl the truth or that she would discover it before it was too late? Did they hope the boy would be different given the love of a good woman?

When a marriage like this ends in heartache for everyone involved, often including children, how does this person, who could have spoken out and possibly prevented the union, feel?

If you are asked, and do not want to say anything negative, ask a Rabbi to call the inquirer and mention what you know or suspect, without using your name. You or someone else can also call anonymously, mentioning your suspicions. The obligation to let someone know about a major flaw which casts doubt on a person's ability to function as a spouse, or a hereditary illness is included in the prohibition of *Lo Saamod al Dam Rei'echa* (Do not stand by while your brother's blood is being spilled). One may be evasive in other areas, but in these circumstances it is our obligation to inform those involved, (even if they themselves have not inquired.) However, you must be careful. If you are positive of your information, tell him so. If it is just a suspicion or a rumor you heard, first investigate it yourself. If you feel there may be some credence to the rumor, make it clear to the inquirer that, although it might be true, this may be a rumor someone started.

People often hide their real selves. Therefore it is crucial to learn as much as you can about someone from the most reliable people you can find; additionally you should get to know him as well as you can in as many situations and under the most circumstances possible. My grandfather use to tell me that, you know 1% about a boy before you get married and you learn 99% after you get married.

Sam married Freeda who was on medication for manic depression. Freeda's parents tried to hide this from Sam. Because the doctor told Frieda to go off the medication for her wedding, Freeda was off the wall. It was soon discovered that without her medication Frieda could not function properly, but with it, she could not conceive. They were divorced before the end of *Sheva Brachos.* Who are we to judge this girl's parents, but unfortunately both Freeda and Sam got hurt.

Rena married a boy who requires medication to keep himself relaxed. Would she have married him, had she known what he is like when he is off the medication? Maybe yes, maybe no, but she wishes she had known, so she wouldn't feel fooled by him and his family. Although she may have married him anyway, she feels it was her right to factor that bit of information into her decision, so she could have married him with her eyes open.

Linda recommended her nephew for my daughter, telling me he was great. They never dated and he married someone else. When I asked Linda about another boy, she enthused about him. Making a comparison, she said he was so easy going, whereas her nephew was extremely stubborn and set in his ways. Why hadn't Linda told me he was stubborn and set in his ways, when she recommended her nephew originally?

Ask around to find out what circles the boy is in, who his friends are, and whether or not he is well liked. You can also find out if a boy gets along with his various *Chavrusas.* This is an important indication of a person's personality. It's a bit late to discover by the *L'chaim* that the boy has no close friends or close relationships.

Make sure the person you are questioning really knows the boy or girl you are investigating. I asked someone if she knew David. She answered, "Sure, I know him well. He's tall and blond. Another person who also claimed to know David well said he was very short and dark. A slight difference...

Two other people and I were discussing the prospect of fixing up a girl. Our conversation sounded like this:

First person: "Oh, she is so upbeat."

Second person: "Yeah, but she's not smiley."

First person: "Yes, but she's so lively and she wants to get married."

Second person: "What? She seems so passive. Her friends seem to want to get married but she seems content to wait."

These were two bright, intelligent women who had both met the same girl. After listening to them, I said, "She's an upbeat girl who's not smiley, who is either dull or lively and either does or doesn't want to get married. Thank you so much for the information!"

People also tend to exaggerate. Everyone is gorgeous. Everyone is great. Everyone has a wonderful family. Someone advised me to drop some of the zeros off any amount of money you hear someone else has.

Halachically, the common practice of inaccurately reporting a person's age is not considered dishonest in a society or situation where one is expected to do so. In other instances, where that information will be taken at face value, you must be precise. Where there is a question a *Rav* should be consulted.

It is appropriate to mention if a boy has a beard or mustache if you are consulted. Girls are more comfortable knowing this in advance. There are differing opinions whether or not to mention if a boy is balding. Letting girls know the boy's height, helps them decide whether or not to wear heels.

"Are you still engaged to that ugly Krasner girl?"

"Nope."

"What happened?"

"I married her!"

BEING RESEARCHED

The information we have is not what we want. The information we want is not what we need. The information we need is not available.

Be aware that you may be rejected for the most ridiculous reasons. You must accept that this *shidduch* is just not *Bashert*.

It is hard to know the best strategy to follow when you are rejected. If you still think the *shidduch* has merit, it may be worthwhile to have suitable people phone the boy trying to convince him to take the girl out. Sometimes, the boy decides the girl must be desperate and refuses to take her out. Other times, the boy feels it's worth a try, since so many people say she's a great girl. If the boy gets smart and agrees to take the girl out, it may be his good fortune.

Although a fair amount of research is advisable and sensible, people are rejected for every reason, which can make a person insane. Some people will reject you for being too tall while others will reject you for not being tall enough. Some will refuse to date you because you are too well off while others will reject you because you are not wealthy enough. The family is not *yeshivish* enough, or the family is too *yeshivish*, too modern, too prominent, or too low- keyed. The family is too well known or I never heard of them. The girl went to the wrong school or she went to the right school but not for long enough. She didn't make the honor roll or she did make the honor roll which makes her too bright. She's too worldly or too uninformed, too open minded or too closed minded. She's not attractive enough or a bit too attractive. She's too out-going or too introverted, too modest or too glitzy, too loud or too quiet, too intense or too easy-going, too self centered or has no confidence, too cool or not cool enough. She's too heavy or she looks anorexic, she can't sing or she's always singing. She's a poor athlete or she is too interested in sports, she has no family to speak of or she's too family-oriented. Often there is no rational reason for the *shidduch* being turned down. Whatever you are is wrong, too much or too little is no good, and of course no one wants mediocrity.

If someone rejects you, it is not because you are flawed. Don't get discouraged - no one is perfect. Everyone really is too tall, too short, too heavy, too thin, too introverted or too extroverted for someone. Sadly, everyone experiences problems sooner or later. Some people may have parents who are divorced, unobservant, or encountering financial difficulties. Others may have relatives in prison, or there may be illness in the family. Even if everything about the person and his or her family sounds perfect now, this family, like every other family, may be tested by *Hashem* and experience hard times too, unfortunately. This doesn't mean the girl or boy being researched isn't terrific.

The problem is that most people want perfection which doesn't exist. Perfection is what is good for each individual, and you only find out who is right for you by giving the person a chance.

People often decide you aren't worth meeting for various personal and silly reasons. Someone rejected a girl because she reminded him of his former girl friend, whom he said was gorgeous. How do I explain this to the girl I wanted him to date, I asked myself.

Issac rejected Gittel because her parents were separated. Two years later Isaac's wife's parents divorced and Gittel's parents had worked out their differences and were reunited.

Claire's parents refused to allow her to continue dating Joshua, once they became aware that Joshua had a somewhat wild background. Though Joshua had grown and matured, developing into a real learner with wonderful *midos*, and the couple were emotionally involved, Claire's parents refused to allow them to marry, causing a lot of strife and anguish. Ironically Claire's parents set Claire up with other boys who had similar wild backgrounds - they were just unaware of it.

Everyone agrees that people are rejected for nonsensical reasons and everyone criticizes the system because of it. Yet most people do not realize that they do the same thing themselves. Be conscious of this, trying not to reject people for superficial reasons. Focus on the important things, such as good deeds, good values, sincerity, honesty, religious commitment, a fine reputation etc. Furthermore, recognize how painful and frustrating rejection is, and be sensitive and careful when you turn down a suggestion.

"My wife should go into earthquake work. She can find a fault faster than anyone else."

Ways to check

An elderly Jewish lady went to her dentist complaining, "The new teeth don't fit." The dentist examined her mouth, studied her bite, and said, "The teeth fit perfectly." The elderly woman said, Not

in my mouth! In the glass!" Be certain that you are checking out the right information.

Because whom you date determines whom you will marry, people can do more than just ask about a person. When appropriate, you can observe the person for yourself. People have been very imaginative in finding ways to meet or check out a person. Parents have observed the girls they are researching at bus stops, at shul or when out shopping.

It is best if you can observe someone in their natural setting, or interacting with people or friends. A wedding can be an ideal place to observe someone. You can notice their level of involvement, energy, warmth, and social skills as well as how he or she looks.

Ellen heard about a girl for her son, and was told she could see her at a local wedding. Ellen asked her daughter to accompany her to the wedding to see the girl. "How can we go to the wedding? We weren't invited," her daughter asked. Ellen told her daughter it would be okay. "We won't eat. We will just look. Don't worry; no one ever asks if you were invited. Everyone just assumes you are from the other side." They went to the wedding where Ellen happened to know a lot of people. Everyone asked her which side she was from and she said she spent the night saying, "Oh, you know the groom, I know the bride," or "Oh, you know the bride, I know the groom." Ellen has been to hundreds of weddings as an invited guest, and no one ever asked her whom she knew. The one time she went uninvited, everyone asked her. I told her to answer, "I'm here to check out the hall." Hopefully, if the person checks out, she may truthfully require the use of the hall.

I feel sorry for people who are not busy doing research. Whenever there's a discussion about Excedrin headaches, they just stand there like dum dums!

I have a *Chassidish* friend who decided to follow the girl to whom her son was *rhed*, observing how she interacted and behaved. Because my friend was certain her son would marry the girl if she gave her approval, since that is how it works in the *Chassidish* world, she felt pressured to choose the right girl. She felt the decision of whom her son would marry was almost totally her's and her husband's. (If the boy really dislikes the girl he is not forced to marry her.)

Chassidim feel a great need to do their research well. The parents feel extra pressure because they are choosing their child's future. On the other hand, they may find comfort in the fact that their children defer their lives to the experience of their parents.

In this system, the *chassidish* parents meet the boy before their daughter meets him and vice versa. This can be a positive approach since parents may be more intuitive, having more experience in life. Of course, as with all dating, it may not always work because each person usually puts his best foot forward, in these limited circumstances.

I once fixed up Ray and Shana, giving each of them the names of the other's references to contact. Rather than calling the names Ray had given, Shana called one of her own friends who knew Ray and then agreed to the date. When I told this to Ray he was upset. His references had been a two-way check. When Shana called his references to check him out, these people knew to interview Shana and report back to him.

It is sometimes possible to check out a person's appearance on OnlySimchas.com. This works if you know the event the person you are researching attended. Although a picture is worth a thousand words, these pictures can be deceiving since they are often candid and present unflattering poses. Yearbook pictures (or school pictures online - most schools have a website with student pictures) are also good ways to check out appearances. Realize that you are only seeing one dimension of a person; the personality and character traits are unseen.

It is ideal if you or your parents have known the boy or girl and his family for years so you do not have to do research. A woman fixed up her niece with her husband's nephew. Both sides had been to this woman's *simchas* and had met each other often. When the *shidduch* was suggested, they agreed to it immediately. The families were well matched and so were the *chassan* and *kallah*.

When my daughter was young I picked out cute young boys in my neighborhood from good families, trying to keep track of them. Then I began to worry: how they were maturing, growing and doing in school? I even tried to influence my good friend, mother of an adorable son, to send him to a school I felt my future son-in-law should attend. I soon decided it was hard enough worrying about my own kids; I did not have the energy to worry about potential husbands from such a young age. Of course, in Europe this was common and it was a system that worked.

I have married friends who grew up on the same block as each other and whose parents were best friends. They didn't do any research. Though each was aware that the other family had issues, they weren't bothered because they liked the overall picture. They'd rather deal with a family whose issues they knew, than discover the issues.

Interestingly, the reverse often happens as well. Some people don't want their kids dating anyone they know or whose family they know, because they know too much about them. Yetta, who lives in Lakewood doesn't let her son date Lakewood girls because she knows too much about their families. She only lets him go out with Boro Park girls whom she researches, but doesn't really know. Though the Boro Park girls have the same "issues" in their family as the Lakewood girls, she doesn't know what they are, and somehow this gives her more comfort. Ultimately, she winds up with the same concerns; perhaps it's even harder because she doesn't know what she may be getting plus she must share her son with someone who doesn't live locally.

Don't make misinformed judgments based on partial research. Often, we assume if someone's parents are terrific, the children are terrific, but there can be exceptions. A daughter may be great, just like her mother, or she may take after her father who is not so great. A giving mother may have brought up a child accustomed to taking. Parents shape what a child becomes, but other influences and circumstances also enter into the equation. Find out about the person himself. If someone's parents don't have a great reputation, but their child is nevertheless terrific, you may want to give them a chance, or you may decide not to get involved with someone whose parent's reputation is not up to standard.

The advantage of the *shidduch* system is that all parties, including the parents, usually agree that if the couple clicks, it's a Go. Although the system is based on this logic, sometimes parents meet the person and object to the match despite all the research. The rejection may be based on a feeling, an instinct, or for personal, possibly inexplicable reasons. Obviously, research can only take you so far.

Some parents research much less than others, telling their child, "Go out with the boy or girl, and if you're interested, we'll look into him or her." Though this saves parents a great deal of time and energy, a problem arises if your daughter or son likes the person and you don't. Your child will resent that you did not research beforehand. It is much harder to talk your child out of liking someone s/he has met, than to reject a person before the date.

I have often heard stories where people forgot to mention something important about the boy. One *shadchan* forgot that a boy was six foot three and only wanted a tall girl; he fixed him up with a terrific girl who was five feet one. They are now happily married.

Sometimes, either by mistake or intentionally, a *shadchan* forgets to mention the girl's age or weight. Some boys are upset, but other boys, committed to the date and forced to spend time with the girl, find they really like her despite these characteristics.

People can reach a point where they stop doing extensive research, deciding to give the person a chance as long as some good things about him meet their qualifications. They adopt a "Let me see for myself" attitude: "What about the family?" "I'll meet them for myself." "What about the fact that his parents are divorced?" "Maybe that will make him work harder at his own marriage." "What if she never learned in Israel but studied in seminary in the U.S.?" "I'll meet her. If she's as great as I heard she is, we'll study in Israel together."

My wife bought an encyclopedia with three volumes missing at a garage sale. "How can you buy an encyclopedia with missing books?" I asked. "I don't have to know everything," she answered.

Don't Reject A Person Because...

Don't reject a person because your friends aren't impressed. If you are happy, don't respond if other friends say he or she "is not good enough for you". Everyone has different needs. Michelle, an older girl who was not that good looking, was about to get engaged. Though Michelle was really happy with this boy, her friends convinced her the boy wasn't good enough. After they exerted enough pressure insisting she could do better, she broke up, and regrettably did not have another chance to get married.

Often if one boy says no to a girl, it's difficult to convince others in that boy's circle to go out with her, because peers exert the most influence. Ten people might say it sounds promising, yet if one friend is negative, the match is over. This is unfortunate because a girl or boy, wrong for one person, may be perfect for his or her best friend. No one can be certain what will appeal to you.

One person, unhappy with his date, might reject a girl, and then unfortunately tells others not to date her. However each person likes or is bothered by different things. One person may reject someone for a reason someone else finds unimportant. Be careful what you say about someone. You can be *Motzei Shem Ra* because of some little thing.

People say no to a lot of good things, often deciding someone isn't for them based on age. "I don't date anyone under twenty two." Why not find out if this particular girl is more mature than average. "I don't date anyone over twenty seven." What if this boy seems and acts young and all his ancestors lived to be ninety? Don't date people inappropriate for you but do be flexible. If someone is one, two or even three years older or younger than you had hoped for, try it anyway.

Young men and women who did not learn in Israel are often rejected, yet there may be valid reasons why he didn't go to Israel, such as a sick relative or unavailable finances etc. Find out what s/he did instead of going to Israel. They may have studied in a *Yeshiva* or seminary in the U.S.A., which is certainly acceptable.

Girls or boys often won't date someone who went to the "wrong" *Yeshiva*. What if the individual is bright, from a good family, sweet, learning and growing religiously, or is moving to the right but isn't there yet? What if reliable sources tell you this person is worth a date? Many girls and boys still refuse to go out with this person, saying, "I don't want to change or develop someone." Meet the person. Maybe he has grown since leaving the *Yeshiva*. Maybe this person is worth developing.

Some people reject a girl or boy because they typecast the person. They won't date any one from a certain area because they are "Jappy" (spoiled or high maintenance), too *frum,* or not *frum* enough etc. Meet the person if a close relative, a well known *Rav,* or a reliable and caring friend tells you this girl or boy is an exception, differing from the way you have stereotyped his or her area, or that the person has changed, grown or has great potential for growth. S/he may not fit your predetermined mold.

In the final analysis, why a person goes out with you is inconsequential. Maybe his research was positive; perhaps he is dating you as a favor to someone; possibly he has no one else at present, it could be he was feeling desperate or was pressured into the date. How the date progresses once you have gone out and whether or not you wish to see one another again, are the only things that matter.

There would be fewer divorces if woman hunted for husbands with as much thought as they hunt for bargains.

RESEARCH STORIES

I married Miss Right. I just didn't know her first name was Always.

One of my funniest experiences with researching was within my own family. I had heard about a terrific single dentist, and wanted one of my sisters to date him. But my sister was tired of being fixed up and said, "If he's so great, you date him." I was married with a few kids at the time, and didn't feel I made good dating material, so I called my youngest sister and told her I had made her a dentist appointment. "While you are there," I added, "check out the dentist." She called me up after her appointment, "I have some bad news and good news. The bad news is I have two cavities. The good news is he's a nice boy." As it turned out, my other sister already knew him.

But it was a riot, showing us what lengths we would go to in order to check out a boy.

Benji checked out a girl and refused to date her, though many people assured him this girl was for him. Then Benji noticed a girl at a wedding and told his mother, "This is one girl I'd like to date." Sure enough, it was the same girl whom he had refused before. He not only dated her, he married her.

Mrs. Stein wanted me to consider Mira, from out of town, for my son. Mira was staying in my area on her way to Brooklyn. Mrs. Stein suggested I send my daughter to Mira, asking her to take something back to Brooklyn. This would give my daughter, who was close in age to Mira and a good judge of character, a chance to meet her and see if she was appropriate for my son. The idea was a good research ploy.

The nth degree of embarrassment is to look through a keyhole with one eye and see another eye looking back!

Donna said she got lucky. Her brother pointed out a boy to her at a wedding and she agreed to go out with him. However, when he showed up, he wasn't the boy she had seen at the wedding. Nevertheless he was the one she eventually decided to marry.

I once did a thorough check on a boy, described by his *Rebbi* as an outstanding learner. An hour before the date, the *Rebbi* called to apologize. He had confused two brothers, and my daughter was going out with the mildly religious brother who was certainly not appropriate for her. She had no choice but to follow through with the date, which was a waste of time for both of them.

Mrs.Wax researched a girl for her son and turned down the *shidduch* due to family background. A few years later, Mrs. Wax's daughter began dating and she tried to fix her daughter up with a son from the same family. Suddenly, the family background which had not changed was acceptable.

Research makes this process so complex that I considered naming this book, **From Dating to Marriage in 12,000 Easy Steps.**

Do your research to find the most direct way and get the most accurate results. Joseph spent months researching Nila; by the time he decided to take her out she was already married and pregnant.

Here's the proof that women are smarter than men: "Diamonds are a girl's best friend," but "Man's best friend is his dog."

David was thoroughly researched. He was found to be completely immersed in Torah learning and teaching. His goal was to live in Israel, teaching and spreading Torah. He did indeed move to Israel when he married, but not to attend *Yeshiva*. Rather he planned to live near a major university and study International Law. David adjusted his goals to conform to what his wife wanted. He is still involved in Torah learning, but he is not a full time learner nor did he remain in Israel. Many girls had dated him because of his idealism. Other girls had turned down the opportunity to date him, because they were unprepared to move to Israel. Had David married someone else, his life may have followed a different course. Young people can't predict where their lives will take them. They are still growing and deciding, and together they often revise the plan they each individually had made. Research can not guarantee what a person will become. That depends on circumstances, on the couple working together to formulate a plan and of course, on what *Hashem* decides is your place and purpose in this world.

Ari said to the *shadchan*, "Tell me something *Geshmak* (really good) about the girl." The *shadchan* answered, "She lent my sister a gown." Not only did this tell Ari the girl is generous, but also that she must be tall and thin like the *shadchan*'s sister. There are many types of research. This one is deductive reasoning.

In one case, the *shadchan* said to the boy, "If you can fall in love with this girl, do so." And he did. Another *shadchan* told a girl,

"Go out with this man. Give him a chance. Marry him." She also listened.

Mrs. Fine had already picked someone out for her fifteen year old daughter. I reminded her to consider their ages. Unless the boy is extremely mature, he should be a few years older than her daughter if she intends to marry at nineteen or twenty. Thinking of other boys as possible options is also a good idea, I added, because you can't be totally sure about your first choice. He may meet someone else, he may not be ready at the same time as your daughter, or he may not want the *shidduch*, etc.

Renee's eldest daughter married the first man she dated. Though Renee is happy with her son-in-law, she is very nervous now that her second daughter is in the *parshah*. She has learned from experience one can marry the first date, so she wants to present a solid candidate to her child. In this system you must stay focused, checking that each person has the right qualities and qualifications. Of course, truthfully, *mazel* plays a big part in all of it. The letters of *mazel* stand for *makom*, being in the right place, *z'man*, the right time and *lev*, having your heart open and receptive.

A young lady came home from a date rather sad, telling her mother, "Jeff proposed to me an hour ago."

"Why are you sad?" her mother asked.

"Because I did some research and discovered that he is an atheist. He doesn't even believe there is a hell."

Her mother said, "Marry him anyway. Between the two of us, we'll show him how wrong he is."

THE SHIDDUCH SYSTEM VERSUS MEET ON YOUR OWN

A husband told his friend, "If my wife really loved me, she would have married somebody else!"

"Every pot has its cover" is an encouraging saying. However, why don't many pots find their covers? Why are there so many singles and why is this number growing at an alarming rate? Some people claim that marriages are so tenuous these days because people are scared to commit. Perhaps this is true, but there are thousands of singles dying to make that commitment who are unable to find or meet their *bashert*. In the New York area alone, it is estimated that there are over 5,000 Orthodox singles between the ages of twenty four and twenty eight, and 14,000 between the ages of twenty and thirty five.

Perhaps there are too many questions, too much research, and insufficient opportunities. People must be more aware of the problem, more open minded in dealing with the situation, less critical, more accepting and more innovative.

In Europe all marriages were arranged by the parents and the *shadchan*. Sometimes the couple met before the wedding, sometimes under the *Chupah*. Some marriages were arranged when the couple was born, others were set up when they came of age. In America a vast majority of religious Jews continue to follow the European system to varying degrees. The practice of *shidduch* dating has not only become accepted, but is preferred by many people.

The *shidduch* system has many advantages: If you are in demand, or have a good network and the right contacts, a limitless number of people can help you find your *bashert*. For others, the right *shadchan* - whether he is professional, or a friend or relative - can be instrumental in helping you find your *bashert*.

Secondly, by the time the girl and boy meet, it has been confirmed that they and their families are compatible to some degree. Each party knows about and approves or accepts the other. This increases the chances of the couple liking one another.

Thirdly, a *shadchan* or intermediary can discuss the feelings and concerns of each party, smoothing out the differences. (see chapter The *Shadchan*)

Another advantage is that people dating in this system agree to date for the express purpose of finding someone to marry. Therefore a person won't expend time and energy dating someone who has no sincere intention of making a commitment.

Finally, if one party does not wish to date again, he or she can break it off through the *shadchan*. This avoids the embarrassing feeling of rejecting or of being rejected to ones' face.

First woman: "A certain young man sent me flowers this morning."

Second woman: "Don't say a 'certain young man,' my dear. There is none of them certain until you've got them."

Unfortunately, the Jewish world – especially after seeing the discouraging statistics on available singles - is acknowledging that the *shidduch* system, like any system, is not perfect. Research is often over done and unreliable (See chapters Research). Those who do not meet certain standards have a difficult time getting approval and making it through the research process. Looks, age, economic standing and divorce in the family are just a few of the barriers which are hard for people to overcome.

You or someone else may believe an individual is perfect for you, yet you may not be able to convince him to meet you. The pressure many people apply on your behalf may be to no avail. This can happen if you lack something on that individual's wish list, if they heard something about you that doesn't appeal to them, or if they prefer to date others. Though you may feel, "If s/he would only meet me, s/he would realize I am right for her," the *shidduch* system doesn't give you this opportunity.

Some people feel disheartened and "burnt out" in the *shidduch* system, because they are often set up with individuals who are not right for them, despite their research. This may be due to looks, personality or chemistry, which no one except the individual himself can truly gauge.

For these reasons, there are now proponents of the social system; people meeting in acceptable social environments. History reveals that from the 1930s through the early 1990s it was common for many Orthodox singles to meet their spouses in social circles, religious gatherings, and conventions.

The Jewish world, including many distinguished Rabbis and community leaders, have discovered the need to expand on opportunities and other means for singles to meet. *Rabbanim* are encouraging people to open their homes, inviting groups of singles over for a *Shabbos* meal or for an evening together. Lectures or get-togethers are organized, with singles encouraged to attend, in a comfortable and modest way. Some *Rebbeim* have begun to encourage seating singles at the same or nearby tables at weddings, so they can get to know each other in an appropriate manner at a place conducive to meeting one another. At weddings with separate seating, the singles girl's table can be placed within viewing distance of the single boy's tables, so each can view the other, perhaps pointing out someone they might be interested in to a parent, friend or *shadchan*.

Recently, The Invay Hagefen and Gateways organization ran two successful weekends, attended by singles aged twenty five to thirty six, endorsed by the *Agudah* and the Novominsker Rebbe. Fifty girls and fifty boys attended. The *Rabbanim* applied this endorsement to older singles, because they realize the situation is desperate and needs emergency action. Some of the most notable speakers in the Jewish world lectured at these *Shabbos* retreats. All attendees were screened before hand. A married couple sat at each *Shabbos* table, making every one feel at ease. This couple acted as *shadchanim*, introducing the singles and helping them get to know each other. It was done in excellent taste, in a frum manner, and yielded many potential dates and to date six engagements. Three couples are still seeing one another. A second weekend resulted in five engagements. Those who participated were quite pleased.

Those who attended were religiously and morally compatible. They were all within a certain age range, had never been married, and had sent in a bio approved by Gateways. Therefore they didn't feel compelled to do much investigating - an important factor. People met each other as people rather than as statistics.

Sammy is twenty nine and Ettie is five years older. Had a *shadchan* suggested either one for the other, chances are each would have rejected the suggestion. They met at the Gateway's *Shabbaton*, saw each other, spoke to one another and liked each other, despite being warned about their age difference. I attended their wedding. They are a lovely and overjoyed couple who will build a beautiful home together, because all the mundane questions and answers seemed insignificant once they had the opportunity to meet.

Two women met on a plane and became very friendly in ten minutes. They started to talk about their families. One woman said, "My daughter just got divorced from a surgeon."

"Maybe it was for the better."

"Before him, she was married to a dentist."

"No kidding."

"She divorced him to marry an attorney. And before the dentist she was married to a CPA."

The other woman said, "Four professionals? Do you know how lucky you are to get such pleasure from one daughter?"

Many people lament the past when it was common for singles to meet at *shul*, a school function, a *Shabbaton*, or at a hotel like Grossingers, The Pioneer or The Homowack. They met in Orthodox surroundings, in acceptable and respectable locations that had *Yeshiva* personnel and parents on premises. Because of the large number of unmarried men and women, I foresee a revolution in the next few years, with a return to the former order, where socializing is permissible and acceptable - of course with more stringent guidelines.

Many people oppose couples meeting on their own, either because they consider it immodest or because they feel it is risky to meet someone without having all the relevant information. Nevertheless, there are advantages when this system is used, not as a replacement to the *shidduch* system, but in conjunction with it.

When you meet a person you see how they look, act and interact so you can appreciate them for who they are. Investigating their age, weight, economic standing, the size of their house, or their family structure, becomes secondary. Certainly, the color of their *Shabbos* tablecloth, or whether or not they eat sushi becomes totally inconsequential (see chapter on Research). People can begin to like one another, and then find out about the rest of the package in time, when their focus concerning many qualities has changed. They get to know a total person rather than forming an opinion based on hearing a small disturbing ingredient of what may be a super human being.

Everyone was able to meet this way, and someone who didn't meet all of today's rigid criteria had a better chance than now. For example, if a girl's looks didn't appeal to a boy but she was bright and perky, she had the opportunity to show him her positive qualities. He could enjoy her personality and like her despite her looks. In the *shidduch* system, if someone hears that a woman is not thin or a man is a bit large, s/he may refuse to date, despite hearing ten other great things about that person.

This is not to say one should meet in a social crowd if s/he has a flaw in his/her looks, age, education, occupation or family structure. Everyone can benefit from the opportunity to meet in an approved, relaxed atmosphere where the answers are easily available and many of the questions become irrelevant.

Getting to know someone before agreeing to go out often helps one make a more rational decision. You can see how a person dresses, how s/he carries himself, or behaves. You can observe her manners, get a feel for his attitude, her temperament and his sense of humor. You can judge a person's comfort levels and how he or she handles crowds. With what intensity and how often does s/he *daven*? Does he put on airs? Is she fine? Is he aggressive? Is she shy? Is he considerate? Is this someone to whom you are or could be attracted? Is s/he worth getting to know better?

A truthful woman is one who does not lie about anything but her age, her weight, and her husband's salary.

Meeting without having to wait to be set up is a wonderful opportunity for everyone. One need not sit home waiting for someone to arrange a date, which happens in the *shidduch* system; if someone is not fixed up, s/he often winds up sitting home depressed. In this system you can help yourself, creating your own social life. You can go out, meet people, and have an enjoyable time. In my single years, everyone knew they could go somewhere and meet people on *Shabbos Nachamu*. It gave everyone something to look forward to and a positive outlook. I advocate this type of dating for those who have *tachlis* in mind.

Another advantage of meeting socially is that most of the work is done by young, energetic, enthusiastic girls or boys looking for their life-partner, in contrast to the *shidduch* system where much of the work is done by worried, nervous, exhausted mothers.

Son: Dad, is it true? I heard that in ancient China, a man doesn't know his wife until he marries her.

Father: That happens everywhere, son, everywhere!

The more homogeneous the crowd, the easier it is for people to connect in these social settings. In the early 1990s, my sister Laya was instrumental in starting an Orthodox group called *Tismach*, geared toward people who would attend coed functions yet wanted a more religious atmosphere. *Tismach* hosted meetings once a week which began with *Maariv* services, followed by a buffet where people could get acquainted, and ending with a speaker who was usually a prominent Rabbi or leader in the Orthodox Jewish Community. They sponsored singles weekends at the Shaalvim Hotel which had separate swimming hours. They had *Yeshiva* Rabbeim present who gave *shiurim* and lectures interspersed with interactive discussions on such topics as *Pirkei Avos*. They also had *kumzitzes* (sing-alongs) taking place during the *Shabbosos*. The relaxed atmosphere, where people enjoyed sports and socializing, encouraged people to be friendly and get to know one another. Because this group attracted a specific type and a specific age group (twenty four - thirty five) they had a tremendous success rate within a short span of time. Nearly forty *shidduchim* came out of this organization within a little over two years.

Unfortunately, some people are unable to concentrate on only one person at these social meeting places. Smaller, more intimate groups are often more successful for this reason. By contrast, once you are set up on a *shidduch* date, you can both concentrate on getting to know one another.

Of course it would be terrific if everyone met their *bashert* through friends, relatives or *shadchan*im but unfortunately, that isn't happening. Making both options acceptable is the solution for those who are disillusioned with the *shidduch* system. The Roshei *Yeshiva* can draw up guidelines for this type of meeting, while *shuls*, schools and organizations can coordinate the events. *Shadchanim* present at the social gatherings to help make introductions will make it easier and more acceptable for people to meet in this manner.

"My advice to you is: Get married. If you find a good wife you'll be happy; if not, you'll become a philosopher." *(Socrates)*

Another Gateways weekends is in the planning stage. Each of these seminars seems to be attracting more and more singles. Rabbi Suchard of Gateways, recognizing the need for singles to meet, is now organizing events for singles in the twenty to twenty five age categories so that couples may meet before the onset of pressure and frustration. Since this age group doesn't command the same urgency, these weekends will be attended by singles together with their parents. There will be lectures and events designated for singles only.

Organizations like One Israel Fund, run fund raisers for singles which benefit terrorist victims while giving singles a chance to meet. Aish Hatorah runs Speed Dating for Orthodox singles. Rebbetzin Jungreis runs a very successful learning program for *Baalei Teshuva* where many singles have the opportunity to socialize.

Many other organizations are running programs which offer a religious atmosphere and social opportunities. Hopefully other *Yeshiva* and organizations will follow these leads. These events are not intended to replace the *shidduch* system, rather to supplement it.

As long as the person is right for you, everyone should accept it and be happy for you no matter how you meet. Society's goal should be to make the meeting and dating process as accessible and least stressful as possible, with each person dating the way he feels most comfortable, not criticizing anyone else's methods. The more opportunities people are given to meet one another, the easier it will be and the more chances of matches being made.

"I've been on so many blind dates I should get a free dog". *(Wendy Liebman)*

THE SHADCHAN

A shadchan tells a man, "Do I have a girl for your son! She's wealthy! She's beautiful! She's charming!"

"Who is she?" cries the man.

"The princess of York", answers the *shadchan*.

"A princess!" exclaims the man, "she's probably very spoiled, needs lots of attention, and requires lots of upkeep."

"No, no!" shouts the *shadchan*. "She is not spoiled. She is sweet and kind."

"Well, in that case I'll agree to the *shidduch*."

"Fine", says the *shadchan*. "Now all I have to do is get the King to agree."

Anyone who makes a *shidduch* or sets up a couple is considered the *shadchan*. This can be a friend, relative, neighbor, or a professional matchmaker.

There is a *midrash* of two people who were matched up haphazardly. They married. After a few days both individuals returned to their parent's homes bandaged up from fighting with one another. The moral: you cannot take *shadchanus* lightly.

A good *shadchan* is like a good lawyer. He can make or break your case.

Know what questions the *shadchanim* ask and what answers to give. Many of these are already on your *Shidduchagram*. (See chapter "Getting Started.") A *shadchan* may ask you, "What type of person are you looking for? What quality is most important to you in a spouse? What are your goals? What are your best qualities? How would you classify yourself *hashkafically*? etc."

Acquaint the *shadchan* with your priorities and what you are looking for; find out what the other party and his family are looking for, as well. Then you can determine if the *shadchan* is on the right track with his suggestion and whether you could be right for the other person.

The job of *shadchan* or intermediary can be quite time consuming. There is much calling back and forth, making arrangements, and negotiating; but if the match works it is extremely rewarding.

A *shadchan* tells a man, "I have an unbelievable match for you. This girl comes with a million dollars."

"Wonderful," says the man. "Set it up."

"One moment," says the *shadchan*, "I must warn you she is very funny looking. But remember, she comes with a million dollars."

The man thinks about it and says, "Okay, set it up."

"One more thing," says the *shadchan*. "She has very little personality, but remember she comes with a million dollars."

"A million dollars," says the man. "Okay set it up."

"Just one last thing," says the *shadchan*, "she has a terrible temper and is constantly screaming. But, just remember, she comes with a million dollars."

The man gives it some thought and finally says, "Okay, fine set it up."

They get married and a few months later the man returns to the *shadchan* screaming and ranting, "You were wrong! She doesn't have a million dollars. Not only that, but I have to help support her mother, father and six siblings."

"Okay, Okay" says the *shadchan*. "So I was wrong about the money, but about everything else wasn't I right?"

Be aware that a *shadchan* seriously affects both people's lives. Be honest and forthcoming in giving over information. People must trust the *shadchan* to disclose all pertinent information s/he is aware of, which may be important to the individuals dating. (See chapter "Research".)

The *shadchan* must match *Hashkafos* and values. It may be inappropriate for a *shadchan* to ask someone from a well-educated family to take a boy with neither education nor ambition unless she has a good reason for suggesting him. The *shadchan* should consider whether the match is really appropriate for the person you are "rhedding" him or her to, before spending valuable time discussing his virtues. Irene spent an hour on the phone with Rhonda who told her about four great friends of hers, for Irene to consider for her son. After describing how terrific the first girl was, Rhonda reconsidered, "She's not really very bright but she has street smarts." Irene's son is brilliant. After singing the praises of the second girl Rhonda realized, "She's not so pretty, but she could be if she worked on herself." Irene's attitude was, "First let her work on herself." Rhonda listed the great qualities of the third girl and then noted that *hashkafically* the girl was looking for something different than Irene's son. The fourth girl would never consider living in Israel, something Irene's son would like to try. At the end of an hour-long conversation, discussing four fabulous girls, Irene and Rhonda had accomplished nothing.

Shidduch groups are a wonderful idea if they are done right. A group of people present individuals they are trying to help. Each presenter must know as much as possible about the person they are suggesting, otherwise everyone leaves the meeting needing to find answers and very little gets accomplished. You may use the *Shidduchagram* questions (listed in chapter "Getting Started") as a guide. It helps to know the person you are presenting personally, so you can vouch for what you are saying. You should also know what the person wants.

I can't stress enough that everyone should be aware of who is single and get involved in fixing that person up with *shidduchim*.

The longest sentence you can form with two words is: "I do."*(HL Mencken)*

Although some people feel the role of the *shadchan* seems contrived, a great deal of discomfort is avoided this way. Before the date, the *shadchan* calls both parties, pushes for the date and helps direct the research. After both parties agree to the date, the *shadchan* informs both sides and arranges a time for the first phone call or date. After the date, the *shadchan* hears feedback from both parties and whether each will go out again, and then gets back to each party as soon as possible.

The *shadchan* should be a middleman only as long as s/he is needed; in no way feeling insulted if the couple is comfortable communicating directly with each other, without reporting to him. Of course, the *shadchan* can call each party to help the relationship progress. "Hi, how are things going? Do you want me to give him a little push? Do you want me to get a feel of what she's thinking? etc."

The *shadchan* may have to push and cajole to get things moving. This should be done with sensitivity and diplomacy. Blanche was leaving for Israel in one week. She had been waiting months for Ira to come back from Israel to date him. When I spoke to Ira, he wanted time to check her out. I explained that there was no time to do any major checking because she was leaving in a week. "You have to take her out tomorrow," I said. "But I have so many obligations tomorrow and she lives so far away." He countered. "If I convince Blanche to meet you in Manhattan, will you take her out?" I asked. After he agreed, I told Blanche that Ira had lots of commitments but he'd cancel some. Still, he'd never have time to drive to Brooklyn to meet her, but they could meet if she were in Manhattan. She went, they met, they even liked each other but weren't for each other. However, each was glad to have met; though they would have preferred that it worked out, now each could move on to the next relationship.

Sometimes, someone is so set on meeting somebody else, it is worth arranging the date just to help them move on to the next thing. Talia wanted to date a certain boy. Though I didn't think he was for her I felt it was worth a try since she wanted it so much. If it worked, everyone was happy, and if it didn't work, at least she felt she had a shot.

A *shadchan* says to a boy: "Do you want to take this girl out? She's a bit funny looking, a little overweight, has a slight limp and doesn't have the greatest family."

"How can you talk that way in front of her?" asks the boy.

"Don't worry," says the *shadchan*. "She's deaf."

There are a few *mitzvos* where a person is called a partner with *Hashem*. Making *shidduchim* is one of them. I have heard it said, that if you make three successful *shidduchim*, you have an automatic entry into *Olam Habah*. Everyone get to work. Do your part. *Hashem* will do his!

In Maine they tell of an old man walking along the beach with his grandson. The boy picked up each starfish he saw lying in the sand, and threw it back into the sea. "Why are you wasting your time and effort?" asked the grandfather.

"If I left them here," the boy said, "they would dry up and die. I'm saving their lives."

Said the old man, "But the beach goes on for miles, and there are millions of starfish. What you are doing won't make any difference."

The boy looked at the starfish in his hand, gently threw it in the ocean, and answered, "It makes a difference to this one."

There are many singles in the Jewish community who are still searching for their mates. They are wonderful individuals who have not yet found their Bashert. If everyone set up one or two people, it would make a difference. It certainly will make a difference to those who are successfully set up. Even if this date does not lead to marriage, it assures a person that we are thinking about him, and it keeps up his hopes.

Often, when an available girl or boy is mentioned, someone will say, "Don't worry about her or him. S/he can take care of himself." This is not a fair statement. Everyone can use help.

It is normal and proper to ask for a *shidduch* or have someone else ask you about a *shidduch* for their child. Don't think, "They must be desperate" or "They seem pathetic." Rather, realize, "Here is a person whom I should care about. Let me think whom I know for him."

Keep a list of all the singles you meet. It can be difficult to recall whom you want to fix up, however with a list of names on your palm pilot or in your wallet, you can check when you meet someone who is inquiring about being set up with a date. I have heard of two people who have each made over one hundred *shidduchim* in this way.

Newly married couples should concentrate on setting up their single friends. Aware of how difficult it can be to meet someone, they should feel a responsibility to help their friends acquire the happiness they have found.

It is considered *BeKavodik* [respectful] to ask the boy if he agrees to the date, before mentioning the match to the girl, to avoid embarrassing the girl. Even though boys may be quite sensitive, girls are usually more so, since they get fewer names offered to them and feel more pressured by the competition from girls of all ages.

Some people have an excellent feel for making matches. Others introduce so many people that statistically they eventually make matches that work. Still others are just lucky, introducing people who like each other. Whatever the case, everyone should set people up, taking a chance and involving themselves in this mission with an open heart and a caring soul.

A Rabbi rode the train everyday with his *sefer* open, learning intently the entire ride. The African American conductor, collecting tickets, approached the Rabbi, "A girl sits in the back of the train who also learns during the entire ride. Perhaps you'd like to meet her." Out of curiosity, the Rabbi walked to the back to meet her. He married her.

The conductor was considered the *shadchan* and proudly danced at their wedding. You never know who your *shadchan* may be.

A woman complained about a man she'd met. "From the first minute, he screamed and yelled."

A friend asked, "How'd you meet him?"

The woman said, "I ran him over with my car!"

My sister Laya, on a date with Issac, from out of town, realized that although he was a wonderful person, he was not right for her. Sensitively explaining this to him, she asked if she might introduce him to her close friend. "She's perfect for you." Aware that he was only in town for a few days, she called Shana from a public phone "I know this is awkward but...." Shana came over and my sister introduced her to Issac. They hit it off, and are now married nearly twenty years.

This same sister told another boy she had the perfect girl for him if he *ever* went to Israel. Sure enough, he called for the name before he went to Israel, looked up the girl and married her. My sister has a gift for matchmaking.

Sometime the *shadchan* herself is shocked when a particular *shidduch* works. I know someone who fixed up a couple though she believed they would not click; he just felt each needed a date. Now they are dating for life – they are married.

People bump into people all the time. Though you may not think of anyone to fix up, you don't realize how often you hear of someone who is eligible - either single, divorced, or unfortunately widowed. People must be programmed to think, "Who just asked me if I know of anyone?" and refer to his list of names.

Can a *shadchan* make a *shidduch* happen? You bet!

Judah kept telling the *Rebbe*, "The girl's not for me," and the *Rebbe* kept saying, "Try dating her a little longer. She's exceptional because she comes from an exceptionally warm, loving family."

Today Judah will tell you his *Rebbe* pushed him into an exceptionally wonderful marriage.

One of the best *shadchan* stories I heard was of a Rabbi who called Shloimie. "Shloimie, it's your lucky day. I don't know what you did to deserve this, but *Hashem* must be smiling down on you. Wait. Maybe I'm wrong. Maybe you don't go for gorgeous green-eyed blondes. Forget I called. Maybe you don't go for the bright, beautiful, charming type. Maybe I'll fix her up with someone else." I'm sure Shloimie was having heart palpitations and screaming, "Yes, I do go for that type!" The boy not only agreed to the date, he begged for it. Then the Rabbi said, "You know what? Let me talk to the girl. Maybe I can convince her to go out with you."

Lisa was a lovely girl whom Ellen believed would be perfect for her cousin Tully. Lisa's parents were aware that their daughter was in great demand. Ellen, telling them about Tully, wisely said, "Considering how great Tully is, you can imagine his long list of names. I'll tell him about your daughter but it would be helpful if you had other people call on your behalf, and perhaps go somewhere where Tully's parents can meet Lisa." By the end of the conversation, Lisa's parents no longer thought of the other boys interested in their daughter; rather they wanted to put Lisa on the top of Tully's dating list.

Can a *shadchan* mislead you? Certainly. People can be persuaded by overbearing, pushy *shadchanim* and sometimes even by subtle pressure. People who lack confidence, are frustrated, or have been looking for a long time can be pushed into an unrewarding relationship because they have been misguided.

A *shadchan* encouraged an outstanding boy with a sick sister, to marry someone totally inappropriate for him. The *shadchan* thought it was a good *shidduch* because the boy had illness in his family and the girl came from a broken home. However, the girl was dysfunctional because she came from a bad home, while the boy was warmer and more sensitive because of his sister's problem. The *shadchan* should not have looked at these people so superficially.

If you want to make a *shidduch*, do it right. Miriam asked me to bring a suitcase back to Israel, where she lived, since I was traveling there from the U.S.. She arranged for her brother Max to deliver the suitcase to Stern College and give it to my sister who would bring it to me. My sister left word for Max to leave it at the lobby desk. When I arrived in Israel dragging Miriam's heavy suitcase she would barely speak to me, because Max had schlepped all the way to Stern to meet my sister and she didn't have the courtesy to come down to meet him. I had thought Max only came to deliver the suitcase, but Miriam had planned to fix Max up with my sister. She should have let me in on the plan.

I know someone who had a terrific son and daughter in the *parshah*. As is common, everyone wanted the son who was an excellent learner, but bypassed the sister since the family was poor. The mother was wise when she told *shadchanim*, "I'll give you first shot at my son if you marry off, or at least fix up, my daughter." Very often you need to use creative strategies.

"Matchmaker, matchmaker make me a match."

There are different types of professional *shadchanim* with different personalities and styles. Some *shadchanim* use pressure, while others are low keyed. Some are great, while others don't come through. Some are quiet and subdued, while others are outgoing and aggressive. Some come across as super caring and sincere, while others truly are super caring and sincere. Some are pushy, while others are laid back. Some can out talk and out argue anyone, while others just listen and say "okay". Different approaches work for different people.

Some professional *shadchanim* specialize in fixing up only Lakewood boys or only *Ner Yisroel* boys. For some boys registering in the Lakewood *Yeshiva*, part of the initiation is meeting with the *shadchan*. Other *shadchanim* fix up *baalei teshuva* or Modern Orthodox. Some specialize in older people. Others only want a wealthy or a very good-looking clientele. Still others fix up boys learning in Israel. Of course some *shadchanim* fix up anyone. Finding the right *shadchan* is essential. It is a waste of yours and the *shadchan*'s time if you deal with the wrong one.

Ask your Rabbi, *Rebbetzin*, the *Roshei Yeshivos,* or your friends who have gone through the process for names of professional *shadchanim* in your area. If you are interested in a Yeshiva University boy, speak to the Rabbeim's wives, asking them whom to contact. (The Yeshiva University boys cannot be type cast. They range from *Yeshivish* to more modern. Specify the type you want). If you are interested in a Lakewood boy or a boy from *Ner Yisroel*, call that *Yeshiva*, and perhaps someone working in the office can direct you to the local *shadchanim* who are familiar with the *yeshiva* boys.

Who is the *shadchan*? The person who thought of the idea, the person who presented the idea, and the person(s) instrumental in making the *shidduch* happen are all considered *shadchanim* and must be recognized as such.

What do you pay a *shadchan* who has made a successful match? *Shadchanus Gelt!* This can range from a Thank You card to a *kiddush* cup to pearls and large sums of money. People give between a few hundred dollars all the way up to five or even ten thousand dollars for making a *shidduch*. Other people determine what the *shadchan* needs, gifting her or him with it. I have heard of people giving candlesticks, silver sets, evening bags, and sewing machines. I have heard of people who helped the *shadchan* pay his debts, his kids' *yeshiva* bills or camp expenses etc.

It is important to know whether a person is a professional *shadchan*, a friend who is being helpful, or someone you contacted because they were friendly with the other party. It is also important to consider how involved the *shadchan* was. Did he just suggest the name, or was he involved every step of the way negotiating, pushing, and making the *shidduch* happen? Though each is considered a *shadchan*, the compensation varies according to their importance and involvement. This is a subjective evaluation. Some times you give what you can afford. Often you must find out what the *shadchan* expects.

One *shadchan* in the *Mir Yeshiva* takes $1000 from each side only if he makes the *shidduch*. Another *shadchan* in Boro Park takes $2000 from the person he interviews, and $10,000 if he makes the *shidduch*. Some people like this because if you are paying that kind of money, you're in a higher financial bracket and you will only be fixed up with others who can afford this type of fee. It is wise to know what a professional *shadchan* expects beforehand. Price is often negotiable. Of course, if you have to pay (a reasonable amount) to find the right spouse for your child, it is a worthwhile investment.

Both sides must give *shadchanus gelt* to recognize the person who suggested or made the *shidduch*. Everyone involved in even the smallest way, should be rewarded with some token of appreciation or recognition. Even someone who went out of his way to call and encourage the *shidduch* deserves flowers.

It may sound more romantic to say, "We met on our own" or "We knew each other as kids," but it is important to acknowledge the good deed a person has done for you.

There have been stories of couples unable to conceive. When they spoke to a *Rav* he asked them if they had acknowledged and rewarded their *shadchan*, emphasizing the importance of this deed.

People are presently working on a new and much needed organization called "Project Marriage". It aims to create a network of trained matchmakers, connecting them appropriately with singles. This could make an important impact on today's Orthodox Singles community. It plans to include a direct nationwide registry of *shadchanim*, and provide mentors and therapists to counsel singles, matchmakers and couples as they go through the dating process. It also plans to provide classes and seminars by rabbis and marital experts. Circulating informational material to inspire singles and address relevant issues is another goal.

The Star K has offered a bonus of $2000 to anyone making a *shidduch* between any boy and a Baltimore girl over the age of twenty two. This is an incentive for people to fix up older girls. Every community and its leaders should try to find some sort of program to encourage individuals to help the older girls find their *basherts*.

I belong to Grooms Anonymous. Whenever I feel like getting married, they send over a lady in a housecoat and hair curlers to burn my toast for me. *(Dick Martin)*

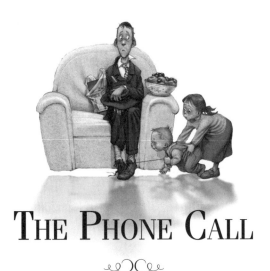

THE PHONE CALL

An aspiring actor called home, announcing with great pride that he'd been cast in an off-Broadway play. "It's a real opportunity, Dad," he said. "I play this man who has been married for twenty five years." "That's great son," enthused his father. "And one of these days you'll work up to a speaking part."

The first phone call can be both tense and exciting.

Usually, the *shadchan* prearranges the date and time of the first call, so the girl need not wait for it, or be caught off guard. The boy, also, after working up the courage to call, won't be told that the girl is unavailable.

On other occasions, the *shadchan* will arrange the time and place of the date, eliminating the pressure of the first phone call altogether.

It's wonderful if the first conversation between the couple is smooth and comfortable, and frustrating if it's awkward with uncomfortable pauses. Yet many couples who experienced terrible first calls marry, while others who enjoyed great first calls meet and dislike each other.

The first call usually is somewhat awkward; after all, you are talking to a stranger. The more you have in common, the easier it is.

Boys often prepare an opening line, such as, "Hi. Is this a good time for you to talk?" Of course the answer should be yes, since the girl has been expecting the call at this time. But it is a courteous opener. You can also begin by saying something like, "Aren't these phone calls awkward?" or, "This is so and so (It's good to know you're talking to the right person). How was your day so far?"

This phone call breaks the ice, and the couple can agree on the time and place of pick-up for the date. On rare occasions one or both of parties wheedle out of the date at this point, if they are really turned off, but that is not right. Once a phone call is made, each should give the other the courtesy of one date.

Had Alexander Graham Bell a daughter, he would not have had a chance to test the telephone.

Some people feel the first call should be short and focused, but there is no absolute rule. If the conversation is going well and you both enjoy talking and learning about each other – talk. Don't talk for hours to avoid investing too much time in someone who may not be for you. A few minutes to one hour conversation is fine. If you've seen the person, or are sure you are interested in him, you can talk longer, getting to know each other. It is advisable not to speak too long, so things don't become too serious too quickly. Trust your own instincts.

"What do you mean we don't communicate? Just yesterday I faxed you a reply to the recorded message you left me on my answering machine."

Prepare lines for your conversation: "How do you know so and so who set us up?" Use the information you know about the other person. "I heard you're studying speech therapy. Do you like it?" (For suggestions see chapter "Conversations Topics for A Date".)

Discuss where you might go, so you will know how to dress. If the boy mentions going out to eat for dairy or meat or just having drinks, the girl will know whether or not to eat beforehand. If he mentions where he plans to take her, she can make other suggestions if she wishes to.

If you feel comfortable, you can give a mild compliment such as, "The *shadchan* said you are lots of fun. I'm looking forward to meeting you."

Say things which you would like others to say to you. But don't come on too strong too fast, because many people are scared by that. Get to know the person you are dealing with and judge what will work for you.

If a date is set, the phone call was a success no matter how weird it seemed.

You know the honeymoon is over when the husband calls home to say he'll be late for dinner and the answering machine explains that it's in the refrigerator.

MEET THE PARENTS

If nobody ever said anything unless he knew what he was talking about, a ghastly hush would descend upon the earth. *(Alan Herbert)*

Proper protocol is important. Following are the rules as they were told to me by friends and relatives:

The boy should be on time; neither early nor more than five or ten minutes late. Of course traffic is often hard to predict, so if you are running late - call.

The boy rings the bell and the father opens the door. One minute later the mother comes in, just to say hello. Two minutes later the girl comes in.

I was told a mother only says, "Let me tell my daughter you are here." I was also told to make only light, low-level chit-chat, simple and non-threatening like, "Where do you learn?" or "Where do you work?"

To help me remember what I was allowed to do when meeting my daughter's dates, I put words to an old song:

Hello, How are you? Won't you tell me your name?

Hello, How are you? I'm so glad that you came

Hello, How are you? I'll tell my daughter you're here

Hello, How are you? My husband will do the *"Farher"* *(testing)*

'cause I'm just doing the greet

It's my daughter you want to meet

So, Hello, How are you? Won't you please take a chair.

Hello, How are you? Now I'm going upstairs…

In other words, parents should not be a factor on first dates.

Of course, I planned to follow these rules, however when the boy walked in, I wanted to make him comfortable but I also wanted to get to know him. Therefore, I made warm conversation, working to put him at ease. I think a good rule for the parents is: talk enough to make a boy comfortable, and give him a chance to talk so you can get a sense of what he is like.

Put yourself in his position, trying to help him relax. A good meeting with the parents helps make it a more positive experience and a better date for the couple.

Sidney walked into Cheryl's house the first time to find his future mother-in-law on a ladder changing the hall light bulb. He said, "Please let me do that." Cheryl's mother immediately knew she wanted this boy for her daughter. Sidney said being allowed to change the light bulb made him feel comfortable right away. You never know what works. There is no set rule.

Though I was told the father must be home to open the door the first time his daughter dates a new boy, this can be impractical if the father works late or far from home. My husband was racing out of the office too often and it interfered with business. After a while, either I or one of my kids opened the door. It worked. I even discovered that the boy was often relieved. If my daughter was interested in the fellow, my husband made an effort to be home the next time.

Often, despite the research, the girl or boy may be disappointed when one sees the other. Nevertheless, one must retain his or her composure, acting polite and concealing the disappointment; go on the date with an optimistic attitude, and don't be too quick to judge.

All a bachelor has to do to discover his hidden faults is to get married.

I was told there is no requirement to do a *farher*. However in some circles fathers *farher* the prospective son-in-law for a long time, asking really tough questions. This is a personal preference.

A girl jokingly said she'd like to rent a father, because her father, trying to be cute, often embarrasses her when her date comes.

The boy is meeting prospective in-laws. Barry loves to tell a *vort* (word or *Dvar Torah*) to the boys who date his daughter. The boys like him, but did he learn anything about the boy? Can he help his daughter make a decision?

One father thoroughly tested the boys by showing them paintings, such as men in *talleisim* looking at the moon, and asking, "What do you think that picture is about?" The boys often guessed correctly that it was depicting *Kiddush Levanah* but could not explain why the men were garbed in *talleisim*. He liked to see how the boys reacted to being tested – not only whether they got the correct answer. A psychologist gave prospective sons-in-law Rorschach tests. Other fathers test the boys on a *blatt* of *Gemara* or on laws of *kashrus* etc. Fathers should do what they feel most comfortable doing, remembering not to be too harsh a judge. It often takes people time to loosen up. Give a person a chance.

I was told to keep a quiet controlled environment, with my other children upstairs, but I didn't confine my kids to their rooms. I wanted the boy to get some sense of what our family was like. I did ask the kids to tuck in their shirts and look presentable. I also asked them not to overwhelm the poor boy. People often hide other pretty sisters not to distract the boy or confuse him.

The house should be tidy.

Dress however you feel most comfortable, without over or under dressing. Though I was warned not to wear sneakers, I would not list this as a rule.

If possible, give the girl a chance to form her own first impression without telling her your opinion at this time. This is difficult and mothers often find themselves telling their daughter "He seems so reserved," or "He's very skinny." Let your daughter think for herself. Perhaps he will appeal to her despite these things.

Behind every successful man is an amazed woman.

Books on proper etiquette say a girl should wait only five minutes and then meet the boy. The boy is also nervous and does not appreciate being kept waiting.

Some people put out nuts and raisins, cookies, or fruit, though most boys are usually too nervous to eat. Offer him a soda because he's probably dry from being so nervous, but don't overdo it and spend your day preparing a banquet. It's nice to offer a boy some form of refreshment but he'll usually take only one cookie, and that's to be courteous. This is just a gesture on the part of the girl's parents and the boy.

If the boy came from far away, give him a chance to use the rest room, saying something like, "Would you like to freshen up?" He'll appreciate it.

Some parents are even more uncomfortable and uptight than the boy. Some daughters want their parents to get to know the boy. Others just want to get out of the house without too much fuss.

Do what works for you and your child.

Make a boy feel comfortable. Show approval. Say things like, "I heard great things about your family." It's a win-win tactic, and has a domino effect. It loosens the boy up and then he'll put you more at ease.

Everyone involved in this initial meeting should realize it is just that - an initial meeting. Don't judge anyone too quickly. It's an unrealistic setting and perhaps both parents and the boy were misadvised, and therefore act too cold, too tough, too aggressive, or too confident. Truthfully, everyone feels nervous.

The Businessman's daughter married a young man who didn't seem qualified to do anything. The manufacturer gave the young man half of his business to enable him to take care of his new bride. Then he asked the young man if there was anything else he could do to make life easier for the newlyweds. The young man said, "Yes. Buy me out!"

THE RULES

A woman goes to a doctor. The nurse insists she get undressed.

"But, I only want the doctor to look at an ingrown toe nail."

"Our rule is that everyone gets undressed," replied the nurse.

"That's a silly rule," grumbled the patient, "making me undress just to look at my toe."

"That's nothing," growled a voice from the next cubicle, "I just came in to fix the phone."

Who designed the *shidduch* rules?

When you first start dating, everything goes "By the Rules." As frustration sets in, rules are bent; people become less *midakdek* with them and many are explained away.

Ideally one dates one person at a time, the person was thoroughly researched, and his references and reputation match almost everything you want. As you go out more often, you realize that although many of the rules are helpful and well worth following in order to bring about this ideal, some rules are extreme, making the dating process more difficult and eventually wearing out the parents and the child.

"It's not done - it's not proper- it's not protocol." The only rule is that there are no absolute rules, and nothing is a law. The following rules are meant to be guidelines. If they work for you, in your circle and in your situation, then by all means, follow them.

The only rule that people should treat as law is being sensitive of other people's feelings in every aspect of the dating system.

The basic rule and foundation of the *shidduch* system is that a boy can't call or approach a girl himself. They must have an intermediary. (Actually people sometimes meet and interact at work, at friend's homes, at school etc. This type of meeting may have its place.)

When a boy is suggested to a girl, an excellent rule is for the girl to look into the boy, after the boy agrees to the date. Because boys seem to have many more choices, it can be futile for a girl to spend too much time researching the boy until he's agreed to the date.

There is a lot of protocol for the first date. Everyone has heard something about it, yet, like The Doctor Spock book, some people use it as their bible while others say, "Who cares?" Some people can't stand if you break the rules; others admire you for breaking them or at least not taking them too seriously.

The following incident illustrates the benefits of sometimes disregarding the rules. Sherri's friends chided her for doing everything wrong on a first date. Sherri offered to meet her date in the city, to save him traveling time. (Broken rule: The girl does not meet the boy, he picks her up.) In order to change the time Sherri called the boy on her own, without notifying the *shadchan*. (Broken rule: The girl does not call the boy for any reason. Any change goes through the *shadchan*). Sherri told the boy she would speak to him the day of the date to let him know what time she could meet him. (Broken rule: The time of the date is determined on the first call). She made up to meet him Sunday at three o'clock. (Broken rule: Don't choose a weird time for a date.) Furthermore, at the end of the date, Sherri said she had a great time and wondered if they had to go through the *shadchan*. (Broken rule: Don't communicate your feelings to one another, only to the *shadchan*.) Finally, the boy drove her home and never even met her parents. (Broken rule: The boy meets the girl's parents on the first date.)

The boy loved it! He enjoyed her and found the experience was less pressure for him. He appreciated Sherri's willingness to meet him since she lived far from the city. He felt it was fine to meet her parents on a later date as long as it didn't bother her parents. He liked her relaxed nature. It worked for them. This doesn't mean it would work for everybody. Do what works for you and your date. However, be careful that you are accurately assessing the feelings and respect for protocol of the other person.

Advice is the only commodity on the market where the supply always exceeds the demand.

Many people object to the idea of going out only once. They feel a second date is always advisable; it is a courteous thing to do, since people may be uncomfortable the first time they meet. This may be a good rule to follow but when you know this person is not for you, one date can be sufficient. Don't waste the other person's time or raise their hopes.

Don't discuss who you are dating with your friends. Though sometimes they can be great at judging who is good for you, other times they are off the mark. Furthermore, they may subconsciously base their advice on envy or on fear that you may move on before them.

N.R.T.G.M. means Not Ready To Get Married. If this applies to you, don't date yet. You might hurt someone.

Don't completely embarrass yourself or lose your sense of pride in order to get a *shidduch*. Remember that G-d is *mizaveg zivugim*.

Some people don't use first names on the first few dates, feeling it is too intimate. They use a person's name after deciding they like each other. Calling someone "Hm hm" a whole night is not my style. I believe in breaking this rule.

When a girl starts calling a man by his first name, she may have her eye on his last name.

If a girl or boy is set up with some one, and s/he sees or hears something bothersome about him after agreeing to the date, go on the date out of courtesy anyway, unless it is something terrible.

You can resume dating someone you have dated in the past, even if you've gone out with other people in between, but only if you are pretty sure this could be it.

To many people, the fourth date means it's time to start thinking seriously before going out again. I believe in dating much longer, getting to see each other in different situations. If it takes six, seven, or even ten dates to be sure that this person is for you, keep going out; do let the other person know how you feel so s/he does not get hurt unnecessarily. Some *Rebbeim* say people must date for at least two months before they get engaged. It is certainly beneficial to date long enough to know each other well, and be sure of what you are getting. Because time is so precious however, don't waste each other's time if there is no possibility of potential.

One boy's mother insists the girl agree to meet her and her husband, if the couple reaches a third date. This sounds like a good idea. Why shouldn't the boy's parents have as much say and influence in whom their son dates as the girl's parents do? However, this can make the third date too important and frightening, feeling like a commitment. Therefore, it should be a rule that both girl and boy meet the other's parents in the early stages of dating, without feeling any commitment.

It is to the girl's advantage to meet the boy's family, seeing what they are like. Because it is common for people to take after their parents and be influenced by them, meeting the boy's parents is an integral part of getting to know the boy. It is also good to be exposed to the family dynamics, seeing where and how he lives, etc.

In fact, it is to everyone's advantage for the boy, girl, and both sets of parents to meet. Why should a girl be nearly engaged before she sees her future in-laws? When you marry, you acquire not only a spouse, but an entire family.

It is becoming accepted for the boy's parents to meet the girl and her parents on the first date. The boy's parents accompany their son to the girl's house on the first date, they speak together for about fifteen minutes and then the young couple leaves. The boy's parents leave a few minutes later.

Sometimes the parents, boy, and girl meet in a hotel lobby, getting to know one another on the initial date. Of course, this can be overwhelming for the parents if a boy dates a lot. Usually, these families thoroughly research each other, so the chance of success is pretty good. These people feel that even if they must accompany their child on numerous first dates, it is smart for everyone to meet and know if they are compatible.

Some kids may oppose the idea of their parents meeting one another, or the girl meeting the boy's parents before the couple is very serious, since this has not yet become protocol. But a joint meeting of everyone, at a point where some interest is developing should be instituted as protocol.

A woman complained to the marriage counselor, "My husband's family always tries to push their way

in. Even in the beginning, they wanted to be in the wedding pictures!"

When Lydia was meeting the boy's parents, her mother asked her if she was nervous. Lydia wisely answered, "Why should I be? I want to like them and I'm sure they want to like me – so it will be fine." She was right.

Sometimes, if the girl's parents are not aware of the *shidduch* system, they don't meet the boy until it is serious. They are missing an opportunity to become involved and give important input. They don't realize how quickly things can move. It is better to get involved early on, when feelings are more casual and less intense.

Wife: You're always wishing for something you haven't got.
Husband: What else is there to wish for?

When two potential candidates whom you are interested in say yes at once, you have a major dilemma. Some people date one person, trying to stall the other. Though some people think this is unfair, if you tell someone you're not available, he will date the next one on his list; it may be too late if you realize after one date that you are uninterested in your first choice. Some people don't want to take this chance.

Can you date more than one person at a time? Protocol dictates that you should not do so. This is a controversial and delicate topic but the question arises fairly often.

Ideally, one dates one person at a time for a number of reasons:

1. It is easier. By concentrating on one individual, you can decide whether or not s/he is for you.

2. It is courteous. How would you feel if your date saw another person while he was dating you? It's nice to feel someone is only concentrating on you. This is not a law, it's a courtesy. In the past,

dating more than one person at a time was called competition and was not uncommon. One of my relatives, one of the original Lakewood *Talmidim*, often dated one girl in the morning and another one at night when he was ready for *tachlis*. Being efficient, he wanted to find his *bashert* quickly to return to his learning. Nevertheless, this one-at-a-time system does have advantages.

3. It is less confusing. Often, if you date more than one person at a time, you can't remember which stories you told each one, or whom you agreed to speak to or date on which night.

4. It is less nerve wracking and you feel less pressure. You aren't nervous that one person you are dating will find out about the other.

If one-at-a-time is the ideal method, why do some people date two at a time?

There are various unusual circumstances, which can lead an individual to date two people at once:

Sometimes people go through dry spells where they have no dates. Then when it rains it pours; they suddenly have too many options and don't know whom to select.

Some people are in great demand. With so many options, it is hard to make a decision. They go out with one name on their list but feel pressured when another great name becomes available.

Others get very few dates, so when a second name comes up they seize the opportunity.

Sometimes the sense of urgency to find someone and be finished with the dating process inclines a person to date as often as possible.

Given these cases, it is helpful to note that there are situations in which some (though not many) people consider it acceptable (though not advisable) to date more than one person at a time. We can understand why these *heteirim* came about, but they can cause complications. The following is a list of popular *heteirim*, which are often forgiven. These are not being promoted, and note that they are not accepted by everyone:

The "Foreign *Heter*": You may have committed to date someone or gone out once or twice with him, when you are told that someone from another country will only be here for a short time. If you don't agree to date him now, you will lose your opportunity. Should you agree? You can because of the "Foreign *Heter*." This has also been termed the "N.Y. *Heter*": Someone arrives in N.Y. from out of state. You can call it the "Cleveland *Heter*": If you don't meet the person now he will date someone else on his list, and then head back to Cleveland. (or Chicago, Baltimore, L.A. etc.)

This is similar to the "Out Of Towner *Heter*": Someone coming in to N.Y. from out of town has a *heter* to date as many people as possible in one visit. People have gone on five dates with as many people in one week. This heter also applies if you visit a foreign country and a rare opportunity to meet someone arises, though you are already dating someone else.

There's the *"Rebbe Heter"*: A prominent *Rebbe* suggests the *shidduch*, so it's *Bekovedik* to the *Rebbe* to go out with the person he suggested, though you have committed yourself to someone else.

Once it's gone this far, why not consider:

The "Unexpected *Heter*": You agreed to date someone, but another boy/girl you've been waiting for, is suddenly, unexpectedly on the scene. You may date both.

The "Cute *Heter*": Though you are dating one boy or girl, someone shows you another cute boy or girl whom you would like to get to know. You don't have to stop seeing the first person in order to date the second.

The "Indecisive *Heter*": Indecisive people may find it helpful to date more than one potential candidate at a time. This enables them to compare qualities (or it may make them more indecisive).

The "Curiosity *Heter*": When two great names come up at once, if you date one, you will think about the other, so it is better to date both.

On a more serious note, everyone has experienced some frustration from this system. You can wait forever to be on a person's list, or you may not find anyone who interests you. When you agree to go out with someone, you are told that the boy or girl who sounds like your ideal just arrived from Israel. Sometimes you wait months to date a particular person, and s/he is available just when you've agreed to date someone else. If you don't go out with him now, he will date the next person on his list. In these circumstances, when you worry about losing a "once in a life time" opportunity to meet the person, you might consider dating two people at one time. That's why it's important to be aware of the above mentioned *heteirim*, though it's better if you can avoid using them.

Dating two people at once is stressful and potentially hurtful, but in rare cases it makes sense. In any case, it is important to focus on the person you are dating at the time. Give him a strong chance but don't prolong it if it seems wrong and you are passing up other options. Avoid prematurely throwing away what you have, for someone else who sounds good on paper.

Despite the instructions protocol provides, people must do what they deem appropriate or necessary in their personal circumstances.

Marriages may be made in heaven, but most of the details are worked out on earth!

THE DATE

My wife and I were happy for twenty years. Then we met.

It is ironic that everyone advises you to be totally at ease, during one of the most intense times of your life.

A *Rebbetzin* once told me that a *shidduch* date is imbued with a ritual spirit. The couple is there for *Tachlis*. It is a life mission and diametrically opposed to looking for a casual friend.

A boy at a party notices a Jewish woman he would like to meet. He tells the bartender, "Bring that woman a drink so when I approach her, she will want to go out on a date with me." The bartender does so.

The gentleman approaches the woman and after a while she says, "What do you say we leave this party?"

"Great," he says "Where to?"

"We'll pick up my mother, go shopping, and talk about medical school."

When should you go out? A *shadchan* usually arranges the date, time and place of the date or phone call, during which the couple themselves orchestrate the date. It is best to go out when it is convenient for both parties.

Consider where each person lives, how far the drive is, and where you are going. If a boy is coming to N.Y. from Baltimore, he may leave after his morning *shiur*, go out at five, and end the date at ten, so he can drive back that night.

Don't schedule a date the night before a big exam when you can't concentrate on the date. Don't schedule the date if you have stayed up the entire night studying for a final or preparing a presentation for work. Don't schedule a date on a Saturday night when *Shabbos* is over late, unless you live near one another. Whenever possible, schedule the date when both parties are relaxed and not too tired from traveling or working. Relaxed, rested people are more apt to have a positive dating experience.

Planning the logistics of a date can be a creative challenge. The time of the date, where to meet, where to go and what to wear are only a few of the considerations. A boy must figure out a means of transportation, get directions, and find out where to park, how much to tip and how much to spend. The boy should always have the girl's phone number with him in case he can't find her house. He must have money, gas in the car, I.D. (license), credit card, automobile club card, E-Z pass, phone, car service number, directions and names of places to go.

Many people prefer dating outside their neighborhood before the relationship is serious. Dating and being seen on a date in a large city is fine and not automatically assumed to be serious, whereas being seen in a small town often invites talk.

My cousin took each of her brothers on a practice date before they began dating. She acted like the date, making them do everything from picking her up at the door, meeting her parents (their parents also role played), and taking her out including parking, ordering, tipping and making conversation. All night, she showed her brothers the right things to do, explaining what a girl expects, such as having the door opened for her. By their first date her brothers were already experienced and comfortable daters.

Even if the girl lives far away, the boy should pick her up. If there is a time constraint or picking her up is very difficult, the girl can offer to meet him somewhere, but this is optional. Then the boy can drive the girl home and meet her parents.

Although it is preferable to date from your own home, some people don't, either because they live far away or would like privacy from their neighbors. Sometimes, people feel it is more convenient to meet in the city or at a relative's home even for a first date. The boy can meet the girl's parents after mutual interest is determined.

Despite the secret planning, it often seems that everyone finds out, everyone tells, everyone sees, and everyone becomes a detective figuring out whom their friends are dating. Everyone goes to the same few places. It is like a Jewish underworld, with everyone trying to hide whom s/he is dating. I always expect to walk into a hotel lobby and see two hundred couples hiding from each other.

Linda was going on her first date and didn't want anyone to know. By mistake the boy rang the bell next door, where Linda's best friend lived. There went the plan for secrecy. *"A Mentch tracht un G-t lacht"* ("Man plans and G-d laughs").

If the girl attends Stern College for Women, some couples prefer meeting on corners, rather than in front of the building, where everyone may see them. I'm told there are lots of corners. I can't imagine there are not twenty girls on every corner and loads of boys trying to identify their date, but I've been assured the system works.

"It is so sad. I have been shopping for twenty years and I still don't have a thing to wear."

Right-wing boys tend to wear suits with ties and black hats. Other boys may wear sweaters or sports jackets as well as suits. Different clothing is considered appropriate in different circles. Girls can wear sweater sets or a suit or dress. Wear what is comfortable for you, as long as it is appropriate.

The boy and girl should determine the type of place they are going to, before the date. By doing this, you ensure that the couple dress appropriately and equally. You don't want one party to wear something formal, while the other is dressed casually.

Girls need not carry a purse if they don't want to, but every girl should take some money, a phone and a license or form of identification.

A boy will wear a hat, depending on what *yeshiva* and circle he is in. In most instances, even if you wear a hat, you can take it off, leaving it on the car seat. Do what feels right for you.

Should one go to a "fun place" or a quiet "getting to know each other" place; a relaxed, comfortable place or a more formal setting? Some people say you shouldn't go to carefree, more "romantic" places like fairs or parks on the first few dates because you have a good time from the fun atmosphere, but don't get to know the person. A quiet place like a hotel lobby, restaurant, or airport lounge is more appropriate. You can begin dating in more formal places, moving to more comfortable locations as you become serious; or you can start with comfortable places if they make you feel more at ease, moving to quieter, formal places as the relationship progresses. Whichever style appeals to you is fine.

Boys can ask if the girl prefers a certain place or give her options. Girls do like options, especially since they often wind up going on multiple dates to the same place. The girl need not answer, "Where ever you'd like to go."

Boys: Be polite and open the car door (and any other door) for the girl. I've heard boys complain that girls have opened their own doors all their lives, so why are they suddenly so helpless? It is a gesture. Men should be smart and just do it!

Once inside the car, a girl should open the car button for the boy, especially if the button release is on her side, unless the boy has a remote key with an unlock button. However a boy should not hold it against the girl if she is unable to lean over to open the car door because of modesty.

Do wear seat belts. It is ridiculous to question whether a seat belt across a girl's chest may be immodest. Safety comes first. If the boy is uncomfortable seeing her with a seat belt, he should keep his eyes on the road. He can look at her when they are out of the car. Seat belts save lives.

How come the Jews wandered in the desert for forty years?
Because they were led by a man and men refuse to ask directions.

Men should know the directions to where they are going.

I once dated a boy who couldn't find the address of the place he planned to take me. He walked me up and down Manhattan for over two hours in freezing weather. When I told him to ask directions, he finally asked a ninety year old, blind man, selling newspapers for the directions. Needless to say, the man didn't know. I was frozen but tried to stay up-beat and encouraging. When he called for another date the next day, saying he now knew where we were heading, of course I sweetly declined.

Married men can't understand why every bachelor isn't a millionaire.

Dating can be an expensive proposition, especially if you date often or for a long time. A boy need not feel pressured to spend more than he can afford. If he can afford an occasional dinner in a nice restaurant, the ambiance is worth it. Some people feel you take a girl out nicely on the first date, but skip the restaurant and go less expensive - like to a café - on the second date. Others reverse the order. Before you know if you are interested in a girl, take her out to a café or for drinks, saving your money for a developing relationship. Use your judgment to decide when it will enhance the relationship. Some boys may have a positive feeling from the phone call, and want to start the relationship in a special way; or a boy may feel there is potential after several dates and then take the girl out more elaborately. A third option to consider is going to a nice restaurant for dessert only. Many - though not all - restaurants allow this.

One friend told me that one of his best dates was getting two coffees at Starbucks and going for a walk along the East River. He added that girls have even suggested they go out just for coffee. Two people enjoying one another's company make a good date, not the amount of money spent.

Often, a boy just starting to date, optimistic and eager to impress the girl, spends a lot of money. As he becomes more experienced and realizes he may be doing this a lot, he often, and rightly so, becomes more careful about how much he spends. It is fine as long as you take the girl to a pleasant place and buy her a drink. It is proper to take a girl out nicely if you can afford it. But do you want to date a girl who is judging you only by the amount you spend?

The girl should eat something before the date, if she doesn't know whether she will be taken out to eat. Always stay *Parve*.

It makes the boy more comfortable if the girl eats when she's in a restaurant. If the girl only orders a salad, the boy may be too uncomfortable to order and eat a meal even if he's starving.

What to order on a date:

1. Low to middle price of menu (but not the cheapest so you both become price conscious)

2. Easily sliced or pre-cut meat

3. No sloppy foods - spaghetti is definitely out! (Before the engagement, however, sloppily eating spaghetti together is a must. It reduces inhibitions).

Most first daters never use the bathroom – that's not easy! Be human on a date. You are entitled to go to the bathroom. Find a nice way to tell the other person you are going to the bathroom. "Excuse me a moment. I'll be right back. I'm going to the ladies room." A comedian joked that before he married, his wife never went to the bathroom. Now five minutes into a trip she says, "Please find a restroom." He spends the whole trip searching for a bathroom she'll accept. "That one isn't clean enough, that one has no tissues," etc.

You may bump into lots of other *shidduch* couples at some of these places. Sometimes it's fun, giving you and your date something to talk about. It can give you a good break if two girls see each other dating. They can go to the ladies' room together and talk, while the boys can also unwind and chat.

Always put your best foot forward. Even if you are not interested in the boy or girl you are with, stay nice, because networking is important and everyone reports back to each other. You usually go out with people in the same circle, and if your date doesn't like you, s/he will tell friends not to date you. If the person had a good time with you though you weren't suited for one another, s/he may recommend you to friends. After such a date, think who may be better suited for the other person.

How much time must the couple spend together, once the boy or girl realizes that s/he isn't interested in the other person? Be courteous and give your date a chance. After going for a walk or drive and drinks, one can say, "I realize you had a long day – you're probably tired" or "I bet you have lots of studying and want to get home." Find a way to hint politely, giving the other person a gracious out. If that person also read this book, s/he will understand the cue and respond, "Yes I do have a busy day tomorrow, I'd better be getting back." If the person doesn't get the hint, try saying, "I'm sorry but I have learning to catch up on" or "work for school" or "a tough day tomorrow", etc.

If one person seems to like the other one and wants to be given a fair chance, the other person should be kind, spending a little more time by talking a few moments longer or taking a walk. It costs nothing and is a *mitzvah*. It makes you feel good about yourself and leaves the other person with a better impression.

My son went out with a girl who was not for him. He acted like a gentleman, paying attention to her and making sure she had an enjoyable time. He said it taught him patience and discipline. He felt it was good because it helped mold his character.

Don't do things on dates that you are not willing to do after you are married. This only misleads a person. Don't spend a fortune on your dates and then refuse to take your wife out because it is too expensive. Don't sit for hours with a boy's great aunt and then refuse to visit her after marrying him. Show yourself as you are, so each knows who they are marrying. Don't act perfect; rather come across as real and human. One of my cousins said he always showed his worst side. If the girl liked him at his worst, he could be sure she'd love him at his best. It's an interesting theory but not one I would recommend.

A short date is not necessarily an indication of a person's feelings. He may have received instruction from a Rabbi that it's the "proper" thing to do. The date should last as long as you both feel comfortable. Too short is unfair because it's not giving a person a chance. Too long is long enough to make your parents worry. Most beginning dates last between three and four hours. The length of a date also depends on how much driving time is involved and whether you are going for drinks and a walk or dinner and a museum. It also depends on whether it's an evening or Sunday afternoon date.

Saying goodnight can be uncomfortable. It is best if both people know they will communicate their desire to see or stop seeing each other to the *shadchan,* after the first date or even the first few dates.

Once in a while, in certain circles, the boy will suggest a second date if he is sure both parties had a good time. He must be certain the girl does want to see him again, is comfortable enough to say so and will not be offended by his straightforwardness. It is wise, when possible, not to tell someone face to face that you are not interested in seeing him or her again (See chapter "After The Date").

Don't judge every second of every date. At different times one or the other feels more confident or more insecure. When one side realizes he really cares about the other person, he may lose his cool. On the other hand, if he feels it's mutual, he usually loosens up.

Some people love dating, some tolerate it, and many can't take it. Each new date brings new hope. Each time a boy comes to the girl's door for the first time, each one thinks, "Maybe this one is it."

Most people don't go out long enough to be absolutely certain the other person is right for them. A boy or girl who never dated, or never had a positive dating experience, may be excited just to find s/he can speak to someone of a different gender. The better you feel about yourself during the date, the more positive you feel towards the other person. It is a good sign to feel good about yourself when you are with a person, but be certain you like him, and don't just feel relieved that the date is going well.

Some people hardly know each other after ten dates. Others feel close and comfortable after one or two dates. Go out long enough to be sure that this is what you want, because this is for a lifetime! Being comfortable with each other is essential but there is also compatibility, attraction, common interests and goals to consider. Date until you are certain you meet each other's needs, and that you both appreciate each other's positive traits and accept each other's negative ones.

Keep track of your own feelings and those of the person you are dating. Do not let your heart race too far ahead of the other person's, or you may get hurt.

If this date works out, that is wonderful. If the two of you don't click, you may not be responsible. Don't get discouraged. It takes two people, the right time, the right place and the hand of *Hashem* for a *shidduch* to work.

Eventually, one person stands out and it hits you *"Kaheref Ayin"* (in a blink of an *eye*).

Love is like an hourglass, with the heart filling up as the brain empties.

DATING PLACES

Enjoy yourself. These are the "good old days" you're going to miss in the years ahead.

Use your imagination and there is no limit to the different places you can go, or fun you may create. You can be typical or original as you plan where to go and what to do together.

There are many great options for dating places. A date need not cost money to be enjoyable. You can spend a day in a park walking, picnicking, bike riding, or boating.

You can cover the local sights. In New York these include places like: The Statue of Liberty, The Empire State Building, South Street Seaport and Rockefeller Center . You can take a ferry boat ride or a horse and buggy ride.

Go to a museum to enjoy a cultural date. Art, wax, history or Jewish museums are all enjoyable, and though you must talk softly, a discussion of the exhibit makes conversation quite easy.

I went by the museum the other day and saw something disturbing. They replaced the statue The Thinker with a computer.

Zoos, aquariums and sea-quariums are also great fun.

A frog telephones a psychic hotline and is told, "You are going to meet a beautiful young girl who will want to know everything about you."

"Great," says the frog, "Will I meet her at a party?"

"No," said the psychic, "Next year – in biology class."

Talk to your wife now – the baseball season starts soon.

For some people, sports, whether watching or playing, makes a great date. Playing tennis, golfing or miniature golfing, ice or roller skating, going to a batting range, paint ball, skiing, boating, horseback riding, or bowling are just some of the many exciting options. Most areas have sports clubs and even major sport complexes. Going to a baseball, basketball, hockey, football or even a tennis match is also an option. Choose what is appropriate for you as well as for the person you are dating.

The prospective bride rushed up to the prospective groom on the first tee. The groom, looking at her in her bridal finery, said, "I told you – only if it rained."

Mrs. Jones began to get nervous when darkness fell and her husband hadn't returned from his golf game. When she finally heard his car, she anxiously rushed out to the driveway. "Where've you been? I've been worried sick!"she exclaimed.

"Harry had a heart attack on the third hole," her husband explained.

"Oh, no! That's terrible."

"You're telling me", moaned her husband. "All day long it was hit the ball, drag Harry, hit the ball, drag Harry..."

The circus, the theatre, shows, comedy clubs, and concerts are all good options.

A theatre patron sat behind a woman who kept up a steady stream of chatter as the play went on. From behind her, the patron said, "Lady, I can't hear a thing." The woman said, "I wasn't talking to you!"

"What do you folks think of the musician's execution?"

"I'm in favor of it!"

Opera is when a man gets stabbed in the back and instead of bleeding, he sings. *(Ed Gardner)*

Take a stroll through a botanical garden.

Remember the immortal words of Eve, who said, "Don't forget – I wear the plants in this family!"

Arcades, fairs and amusement parks create light, easy atmospheres.

Places like "My Name is Mud" where you paint and mold clay pottery is an enjoyable option. You must return to pick up your project at a later date, so it is advisable to get a separate ticket stub for each person's pottery or agree to return together. Build a Bear is another fun activity with many locations.

Lounges and hotel lobbies are relaxing places, creating a nice atmosphere to talk and get to know each other; they are also usually inexpensive. Most hotels will allow you to sit in the lobby. It is proper to buy the girl a drink.

Business has been so bad at one major hotel that the management is stealing the towels back from the guests.

Once you are comfortable with each other, drive up to the country, or stay in and play Trivial Pursuit or Monopoly together. How about reading and laughing at this book together?

CoolestDates.com has a list of ideas for all types of dates and all types of occasions in different price ranges. Check this out.

Eating is the most common activity on a date. Whether you go to a restaurant, café, coffee bar, pizza shop or ice cream parlor, eating out is fun for most people.

Before marriage, the three little words are, "I love you." After marriage they are, "Let's eat out."

The hold-up boy walks into a Chinese restaurant and says, "Give me all your money." The man behind the counter says, "To take out?"

Bride: "The best things I cook are meat loaf and peach cobbler."

Groom: "Which is this?"

You can go on line to get a listing of kosher restaurants and their respective *hashgachos*. Type in "kosher restaurants" with the location you require, and you will get a complete listing which includes OU certified kosher restaurants in that area.

A man waits for his friend in a restaurant. The waiter asks if he would like something while he is waiting. The man says, "I'll just have a cup of coffee." After a while, tired of waiting for his friend to show up, he asks for the bill and is flabbergasted when the waiter hands him a bill for twenty-five dollars. "Why is it so expensive?" asks the man. "I only had a cup of coffee." The waiter says, "Take a look around you. Look at the expensive furniture. Notice the magnificent artwork. Take note of the magnificent décor we've created. This all costs money." The man reluctantly pays the bill. The next day he returns to the restaurant again and asks the waiter for a cup of coffee adding, "Remember - for your decorating I already paid."

CONVERSATION TOPICS
FOR A DATE

A smart husband is one who thinks twice before saying nothing.

The major question most people ask is, "What should I talk about on a date?" Some people are natural conversationalists, comfortable even while talking to a total stranger. But many people, especially in a tense situation like dating, are nervous about what to say.

Prepare some topics to discuss. Prepare lines to break the ice. "It's my first date. Please go easy on me."

Prepare stories, questions and statements. It is a good idea to be ready with a few stories that can fit any topic. Decide what you want to discuss and bring it into the conversation.

My mother taught me to prepare an essay to fit any topic, to use for school compositions. For example, I'd write a composition about my friend and his dog. If the assignment I received was, "How I spent my summer vacation", I wrote about how I spent the summer with my friend and his dog. If I had to write about my favorite person, I wrote about my friend and his dog. If the assignment was about my funniest date, I wrote about a date in which I bumped into my friend and his dog.

If conversation doesn't come naturally, or if you are nervous, prepare some cute stories and fit them into your conversation. Prepare a funny story about something that happened in school. If the boy asks about your brother, say he's the type that laughed when you told him what happened in school. Then tell him your story of what happened in school. If he asks about your summer, say the summer was nice but school was a riot, and proceed to tell the same story. If you have a few different stories prepared, they can help you be comfortable until you really are comfortable.

Often people starting to date are inexperienced talking to the opposite gender. If an inexperienced girl and an inexperienced boy go out, both don't know how to communicate. If one is experienced in dating and the other is inexperienced, the inexperienced one had better catch up quickly.

The worst thing on a date is silence. Ask questions you'd like the other person to ask you, such as your goals, your dreams, what you're looking for in a spouse, and how you'd like to raise your children. Ask about the person's relationship with his parents and siblings. What are they like? Are they alike? Talk about subjects with which you are comfortable. Be honest but do not put yourself down. Don't make comments like, "I'm so dumb." It leaves a bad impression.

People often wonder what they can ask. Susan was dating a boy whose parents were divorced. She wouldn't ask him about it even though they dated for a while, saying, "I don't want to get too personal or I will embarrass him."

If you don't ask you won't know. It's hard to ask about divorced parents, or other sensitive family issues, so be delicate but do ask. Get to know the person's temperament and personality on the first few dates; then if you like him, ask the tougher questions. Help make the other person feel comfortable and hopefully, s/he will do the same for you.

Memorize the questions you'd like to ask. Can you pull out a slip of paper containing the questions? Definitely not, unless you are comfortable enough to say in a cute manner, "Okay, let's both pull out our list of questions." Write the questions on your hand (don't sweat) or have crib sheets in your pocket or pocketbook which you can sneak a look at it every so often. I know someone who took his list to the men's room, to check whether he had covered all his questions.

Richard said his problem is, "I don't talk much, I think a lot." In order to develop a relationship, you must force your thoughts to your lips; don't censor everything because you must develop a rapport.

Hashkafah is a major topic of discussion. For people who have moved to the right as they've matured, comparing how much s/he wants to grow and/or change is an important part of their discussion. Be aware that no matter how much you discuss, you can never know what life will deal you and how different events in your life will affect you. It is important to have a good relationship and be prepared to grow together.

The *Rebbe* of my relative's husband advised him to talk about "*shtusim*" (not serious things) rather than Torah on their dates. Before they were engaged, the only thing he said to her about religion was, "I'd like a Torah life." My cousin answered, "Sounds good to me." I know other boys who spend their dates discussing *Divrei Torah* and telling the girl what they learned in *Gemara* that day. It's smart to diversify your discussions.

People discuss broad topics such as what type of home they would like, as well as specifics such as how many children they want and what kind of parent they hope to be. These discussions have value yet they are only discussions which help you understand one another's hopes, dreams and attitudes. Girls who say they want twelve kids are often overwhelmed after having three. Men who think they can only handle a few kids find they want many more. Couples who think they want to live in a certain neighborhood find they can make a living in another neighborhood. These discussions, though hypothetical, give you a better understanding of the other person and his or her perspective on life.

Below are some suggested topics to discuss on a date. Be sure to ask the questions in a relaxed conversational manner; not as if it were a test. Ask the questions that interest you and that will interest the other person.

Topics:

Education - What schools have you attended? Why did you choose that particular school or *yeshiva*? What are the pros and cons of the school? What subjects are you studying or did you study in school? Who are your favorite teachers? What type of student are you? What high school, seminar, college, *kollel*, graduate school did you attend or hope to attend? How long do you want to keep learning? Do you plan to go in to *chinuch* or *kiruv*? Under what circumstances should a husband stop learning full time and start working?

■ *Family* – What kind of a relationship do your parents have with each other, with the kids, with their own siblings, with their in-laws? What are your parents like? (outgoing, quiet, involved, strict or lenient, warm and loving, detached, strong, etc.?) Which of your parents are you most like? How did your parents meet? What are their interests, careers and priorities? What are your siblings like? Which of your sibling are you most like? With which sibling are you closest? How did your siblings meet their spouses? Are you close with your sibling's spouses and their children? How close is the entire family; the extended family?

■ *Yichus* - What are your grandparents like? What are or were your great grandparents like? Did you know them? Where did they come from? Do you know about their lives or heritage?

■ *Friends* - Who are your closest friends? What are they like? What do you have in common? What qualities do you look for in a friend? From where are your best friends? How long have you been friends? Discuss friends you might have in common.

■ *Camps* - Which have you attended? Why that specific one? Did you like it? Were you active in camp? What was your favorite thing about going to camp (color war, sports, trip days, singing, making new friends, swimming etc.?

■ *Career goals* – What field would you like to enter? What made you choose this field? How do you feel about learning vs. working or a combination? Do you enjoy your job? If you could have any job in the world what would it be? Do you think you will be working in the same field in ten years? What changes do you see in your career? How do you balance working toward success and spending time at home? Can (a woman) continue in her field after having children?

■ *Community* - What is your neighborhood like? Do you like it? Why did your family choose that area? What are the people in that area like? Would you like to continue living there after you are married? Which *shul* do you attend? Why did you choose that *shul*?

■ *Interests* – What are your hobbies? What books do you read? Who are your favorite authors? What newspapers do you enjoy? Do you play an instrument? What do you do in your spare time? What do you like to do for entertainment? Are you into singing? Who are your favorite singers? Are you into sports? Which ones? Which tapes do you enjoy (both music and Torah tapes)? How are your computer skills? Do you spend time on the phone? Email?

■ *Shiurim* – What good ones have you heard? Which *Rebbe* do you enjoy hearing? What would be your ideal line up of speakers?

■ *Fun Topics:* What do you think of the *shidduch* system? How do you know the *shadchan* who set us up? What are some of your funniest, unusual or most memorable experiences (including dating experiences)? What are your favorite places to go for relaxation?

Have you ever spent time on a farm? Do you enjoy museums, bowling, skiing, ball games, amusement parks, picnics etc.? Who are your favorite comedians? What are his or her best jokes?

■ **Israel** – How do you feel about Israel? Do you have friends or relatives living or learning there? Would you want to spend some time there after you marry? Would you consider living there long term? If you did live there, which community would you prefer? Discuss common experiences such as your impressions of your study year in Israel.

■ **Organizations** – With which, if any, are you involved? Which organizations do you think are most worthwhile? How involved would you like to be in schools, *shuls*, and various organizations?

■ **Travel** – What are your favorite places to go? What was your favorite vacation? What are the most interesting sights you've seen? Where do you hope to travel someday? Why there? Do you think it's important to visit Eastern Europe in order to remember the Holocaust? Do you feel it's important to visit Russia?

■ **Politics** – (Israeli, American or World Politics) How do you feel about the situation in Israel? What do you think of the Prime Minister's policies? Whom do you think is Israel's best spokesman? What do you think of the President's policies regarding the Middle East? What's your impression of the Mayor? Governor? Senator? For whom are you considering voting? To what do you attribute the growing anti Semitism in the world?

■ **Hashkafa** and **Emunah** – Which *Rav* has had the greatest effect on you? Which *Rav* do you follow? Are you interested and involved in *kiruv*? What is your *Shabbos* table like? What would you like your own *Shabbos* table to be like? Do you enjoy having a lot of guests at the *Shabbos* table vs. privacy or family time together? How important are singing and *Divrei Torah* at the table?

■ **Personality** – How would you describe your personality? (quiet, outgoing, funny, reserved, punctual, carefree, driven, goal oriented, involved, giving, independent)

▪ Of what are you most proud? What do you feel are your greatest or most meaningful accomplishments? What do you find most rewarding? What is your typical day like? What do you like about yourself and why? What is your best quality? What makes you happy? What makes you sad? What would you like to change about yourself? What things about yourself are you trying to work on improving? On what *Midah* are you working? Are you involved in *chessed*? What *chessed* do you feel you do both in and out of home? How ambitious are you?

▪ **Goals** - What are your goals? What would you like to accomplish in life?

▪ **Priorities** - What are your major principles? Do you think you acquired these principles and beliefs from your home, parents, friends or Rabbi? Whom do you most admire? Who is your role model? Who has been the greatest influence in your life?

More serious topics for later dates:

▪ **Marriage** - Why do you want to get married? What are you looking for in a spouse? What needs do you expect your spouse to meet? What are you looking for in a father or mother to your children? How much can or can't you be there for the other person? Do you put yourself or the other person first? How do you settle differences?

▪ **Parenting** – What type of parent do you hope to be? How large a family do you think you would like? What type of children do you hope to raise? Would you bring up your children the same way your parent's raised you? What would you do the same as your parents? What would you do differently? What are your ideas on child rearing and disciplining children (punishment vs. reward)? Where would you want your kids to attend school or camp?

▪ What are your plans for the future? How would you like to spend your vacations?

■ What type of lifestyle would you hope to lead? Who can help support us? (Issue of support- career or *kollel* life) How long do you envision it will be until we can support ourselves?

Discuss how you feel your families will get along.

Discuss your hopes and dreams

Discuss taking *Chassan* and *Kallah* classes.

Discuss engagement plans, the *L'chaim* and *Vort*

Finally, discuss wedding plans.

At this point, conversation should come naturally. You can think of your own topics.

Nine tenths of the people couldn't start a conversation if the weather didn't change occasionally.

DATING STORIES

A husband said to his wife, "I've really taken you over all the bumps of life, haven't I?"

The wife said, "That's true. I don't believe you missed any of them!"

Here are true stories - funny and serious - of people I know personally. We can laugh, but we can also learn that we are all human from them. Not all of our dates are perfect; even the most well planned dates can go wrong. Learn not to judge a person by a single incident. Realize that we are all nervous. All of us have misjudged people or situations at times, and all of us feel we are being misjudged at times. Some things don't work out, no matter how hard we try, and some things work out for the best in spite of ourselves.

Sara was on a date, when her contact lens fell into her soup (hard lenses pop out easily). Too embarrassed to say anything, she just picked up her soup and marched off to the ladies room to search for it. It's hard to imagine what the boy thought.

• • •

One of the most encouraging stories happened to a close relative of mine. Avi dated about twenty girls, each quite a few times, but none of them were "it". One Friday, someone in the neighborhood called Avi's mother, saying his niece Rachel was in from out of town and asking if Avi could take her out Saturday night. Avi's mother had previously checked out Rachel but because of his long list of names, Avi had never dated her. Since Rachel checked out well and Avi did not have a date for Saturday night, Avi's mother agreed to the date. Avi and Rachel went out and by the end of the date announced they were ready to get engaged. They decided to fly to Rachel's hometown, meet her parents, and announce the engagement the following Sunday. Of course by Tuesday, three days after their first date, everyone knew they were unofficially engaged. They are a terrific couple. I tell everyone this story to give them hope. Now you may be lonely and searching, but within a week you may be announcing your engagement. So keep your chin up!

We share household chores. I dry the dishes. My wife sweeps them up!

One frustrated *Rebbe* told me about his date with a very overweight girl. He asked her, "Would you like steak, chicken, a hamburger?" She said, "Okay."

• • •

One boy suddenly realized he had ripped his pants. He made some excuse about buying a gift for his brother and went into a clothing store. He quickly grabbed a shirt and a pair of pants so no one would realize he needed new pants. When he got to the register he told the check-out woman he only needed the pants. The couple then went to a restaurant where the boy, excusing himself, went into the rest room and tossed his old pants out the window. Then he opened the bag, to find that the woman at the check-out counter had given him only the shirt! I was never told how he got himself out of this mess.

• • •

Yaakov was very nervous on his first date. He arranged to pick up a girl from a wedding hall. He had the valet park his car and went in to meet her. When he came out, the girl opened her own door, and Yaakov apologized for not having opened it for her. He got in, laid his coat and hat on the back seat, and began to pull out when he realized it wasn't his car! This car was too dirty. He had been cleaning his car all day in preparation for the date. He said to the girl, "Great, now I get a second chance to open the car door for you."

• • •

It's good to keep your calm and your sense of humor. Unfortunately, things do go wrong. Don't be embarrassed. Just handle the situation. It is important to see how the boy and girl react in these instances; you gain insight into the person's true personality.

Josh told me that he decided not to date a girl a second time, because she spent the entire first date telling him why she would never go out with him again.

• • •

Lester dated three girls in one day. How did one shine out? Baila told him she liked him and pursued him. Lester dated Baila a few times but then went on to the next girl. Baila also dated another boy, but feeling Lester was right for her, she had the *shadchan* keep pushing him to give it another try. Knowing how Baila felt about him made Lester willing to give her another chance. They began dating again and got married. They both are lucky.

• • •

I have a relative who dated one hundred and thirty seven girls. His wife was his one hundred and thirty sixth. She says the first one hundred and thirty five don't bother her. It's that one hundred and thirty seventh that he dated after meeting her, which drives her nuts. "Why did he feel the need to date any one else after meeting me?" she jokes. Of course, he got smart and backtracked to her.

• • •

Emily told me she had a crush on Shawn, a very popular boy. Though she was also extremely popular, Shawn never asked her out. When she got engaged to her husband, Shawn asked him, "How did you ever get Miss Popularity? I was always afraid to ask her out." When Emily tells this story, her husband interjects, "See how lucky she is. Shawn is now divorced, and she is in a wonderful marriage."

Some mornings I wake up grouchy …and some mornings I just let him sleep.

Rita went out with Marshal who really liked her. Though Rita liked him, she felt he wasn't right for her. However each time she called a halt to the dating, Marshal's mother called the *shadchan*, Rita's relatives, or her parents' friends asking them to encourage Rita to keep trying. So Rita kept dating Marshal, trying to make their differences work. On each date they realized their goals and objectives were different, yet people continued to exert pressure and Rita continued dating him. Finally though, Rita told Marshal that he was not for her. Marshal's mother (obviously a very caring mother) called Rita's mother saying how taken aback she was. Rita had dated her son for a while, they had worked through their differences, Marshal thought they were getting engaged, and then Rita had broken up with him! Rita's mother explained that her daughter had tried numerous times to end the relationship, and had indeed given it her best effort. Rita and her mother felt terrible, but Marshal and his mother had ignored the signs.

• • •

Gary parked his car in the city and took his date to a small café. When they came out, Gary couldn't remember where he had parked his car. It was raining, so he told the girl to wait while he searched for his car. Unsuccessful, Gary was finally forced to call his brother to drive him up and down the blocks looking for the car. By the time they located the car, Gary could not remember where he had left the girl. Finally he found the café, but the girl had taken a cab home. What a comedy of errors! Luckily, this girl understood things could and do go wrong, and she agreed to meet him again.

• • •

Ryna stepped out in front of a moving car and was nearly hit when Reuven grabbed her shoulder and pulled her back. Ryna was furious that he had touched her and refused to date him again. Perhaps she thought it was better to get hit by a car, in which case Reuven was lucky not to see her again.

• • •

Danny spent the entire evening telling Raila how their signs were compatible. Because she was an Aries and he was a Gemini they were perfectly in sync. He told her their orbits were tied and explained that their karma was on the same wave-length. Raila smiled sweetly through the evening, hoping that as soon as Danny took her home he would get a sign telling him to orbit to a different compatible female.

• • •

Marty asked Penny how many siblings she had. When Penny said she had three brothers and two sisters, Marty said, "I was told you have two brothers and two sisters." Penny insisted she had three brothers and Marty insisted she had two. When Marty told me this story, I asked him why he was ridiculous enough to argue with her. Obviously, Penny knew better than he how many brothers she had. Marty answered, "Yes, but wasn't Penny silly to argue with me over it?" He enjoyed seeing how a girl reacted to confrontation. Needless to say, she was not interested in dating him again. He didn't care because he wanted a wife who would like him even when she saw his worst side. He happened to marry an outstanding girl so I suppose his theory worked for him.

A man rushes into his house, yelling to his wife, "Martha, pack up your things. I just won the California lottery." Martha replies, "Shall I pack for warm weather or cold?" The man responds, "I don't care, just so long as you're out of the house by noon!"

A boy was told before the date, that he and the girl had to click. At the end of the first date he nervously asked her, "So, did you hear a click?"

• • •

Sam knew this girl was for him because he felt so comfortable being with her, he began to sing in the car on his way home from the date.

• • •

Joseph went out so many times, he brought his one hundredth date candy and flowers. He had a great attitude saying he would continue to give candy and flowers to every one hundredth date.

• • •

Simon dated a girl for six weeks and she thought she knew him well. One day during an argument, Simon slammed the car door on her. She broke up with him. Later it was discovered that Simon's father beat his mother. People often learn from what they see. Try to date a person long enough to know what they are really like, and to what kind of upbringing they've been exposed.

• • •

Jake had theories on women. He rejected a young girl who was very thin, believing she would be unable to bear children. She had fourteen. He dated another girl whom he believed was too fragile and would be too weak to work. Subsequently, this woman had twelve children and worked as a *sheitel* maker, putting in long hours all her life. He dated a girl who was an only child and deduced she wouldn't know how to handle children. She is now married with eight terrific kids. When Jake went to the home of another young woman he dated, her father got himself a glass of water. Jake decided she would be like her mother – no help to her husband. This woman too, eventually worked every day of her life. In fact, when I mentioned this story to the woman's cousin she said, "My aunt always begged my uncle to sit down and let her get him his water." Jake finally married a woman whose mother always worked, believing the daughter would also work. She is a terrific woman but only worked for a few months after the wedding and then concentrated on raising their kids. So much for all his theories! They can only take you so far. You must know each individual.

• • •

I've heard stories of girls and boys being so nervous they vomited on their dates – not fun for either party, but it happens.

Sharon could not get a flight home from Israel. Her mother called a *mekubal* to ask if he had connections with the airlines. The Rabbi told her to have Sharon fly Swiss Air, saying it "would be good". Sharon flew Swiss Air and was seated next to an elderly Belgian woman who fixed her up with her grandson. The flight was good and the grandson was good. Sharon married him.

My wife thinks that I am too nosy. At least that's what she keeps scribbling in her diary. *(Drake Sather)*

Tommy asked his aunt to suggest a restaurant to take his date. She suggested a Manhattan restaurant and Tommy took his date there that night. He was shocked to find not only his aunt there, but also his uncle, their four kids and his grandparents sitting at a table. Though none of them approached him, he kept hearing his grandfather say, "Isn't that Tommy?" It seems his aunt had some big news to break to her kids and parents; the restaurant she had just discussed with Tommy came to mind so she went there, totally forgetting that Tommy and his date would be there. Tommy had a tough time concentrating on the girl but had a good laugh afterwards.

Bride: You're my little peach.

Groom: You're my little plum.

Rabbi: I now pronounce you fruit cocktail.

Gila broke up with Moshe because, as she told the *Rebbetzin*, he was too stingy to spring for a 75¢ can of soda. He married another girl. One day Moshe's wife came to the *Rebbetzin*, "My husband is so good. He said the check I gave you for *tzedakah* wasn't large enough, so he asked me to bring over another one." To think this was the same boy Gila

felt was too tight with money to buy a soda! Perhaps when Moshe dated Gila, he was too inexperienced at dating to realize he should buy her a drink. Judge every person *Lekaf Zechus* (giving the benefit of the doubt).

Shira met Fred who was in medical school. Fred dropped out of medical school saying he wanted to go into business. Shira broke up with him afraid if he couldn't decide what he wanted to do, how could he decide on a wife? She dated other people for two years and finally began dating someone seriously. Suddenly Fred called her and said, "You can't marry anyone else, you're going to marry me." And sure enough, after not seeing one another for two years, they got married. Obviously, he did know what he wanted.

● ● ●

Brenda grabbed the keys out of a boy's car and refused to give them to him for ten minutes. Finally she handed them back, saying, "You passed the test." He drove her home and said, "You failed." Don't test a person. Life sets up its own tests. It is good to see how a person reacts to different situations, but remember you are also being judged. If you are the type who is often late, it's probably better to be yourself at some point and see how the boy or girl reacts to your lateness.

I believe you should live each day as if it is your last, which is why I don't have any clean laundry, because, come on, who wants to wash clothes on the last day of her life?

Jean was set up with Mendy who was much too short for her. Because she had determined he was not for her immediately upon seeing him, she was comfortable and bubbly. Mendy therefore was in shell shock when, at the end of the night, Jean suggested he date her friend Ruth. Though he was hurt, he finally agreed to the date. But when Jean phoned Ruth, she antagonistically drilled her about why Jean had not been interested in him. Ruth, a popular girl in no rush to date a boy who felt jilted, agreed to the date only because Jean raved about Mendy. However, she again questioned and screamed about why Jean hadn't wanted to see him again. Both of them felt used and abused. It is a good lesson. A person must be ready to like another person. Wait until that time. Of course, sometimes people in a vulnerable state are more inclined to get involved with someone new. Try to know the mind set of your potential date.

• • •

Barbara was serious about Steve. He moved into an apartment and she dropped by to see it. She was struck by the way Steve unpacked every box of cereal, rice, grains and beans, putting them in individual jars. When she asked him why, he said, "I don't know, my mother always did it." She figured, "This boy doesn't need a wife and anyway, he is so settled into this apartment it doesn't seem like he is ready to get married and move out. He seems settled into bachelorhood." She broke up with Steve because she wanted *Tachlis*. Years later, Barbara found tiny flies in a box of cereal. The exterminator suggested she put all her cereals, rice, grains and beans in individual jars. Barbara burst out laughing. She finally understood why Steve had done that. It hadn't been a sign of settling into bachelorhood, rather something Steve had seen in his home. At one time, Steve's mother must have experienced the same problem and therefore always placed everything in jars. Barbara had totally misinterpreted the situation. Be careful how you judge a person or interpret a situation.

• • •

Once I was set up with a relative's relative who was not for me. My grandfather, always in a rush to see me married, asked why I wasn't interested in this particular boy. Not wanting to say anything negative, I quickly answered that he was too short. My grandfather said he had an extremely tall friend who married a very short girl. Once, while walking in the street, she fell down a manhole; he never noticed and just kept walking. So why would I want to be with a boy taller than me? My grandfather could find a reason for every boy to be given a chance.

After she woke up, a woman told her husband, "I just dreamed you gave me a pearl necklace for my birthday. What do you think it means?" "You'll know tonight", he said. That evening, the man came home with a small package and gave it to his wife. Delighted, she opened it to find a book entitled The Meaning of Dreams.

THE PERSON

There's only one perfect child in the world and every mother has it.

A non-religious man brings home a silver *mezuzah* as a gift for his Rabbi from Israel. The rabbi, looking at it realizes there is no *klaf* inside. He can't believe the wealthy man would buy a *mezuzah* without a *klaf*, so he asks, "Did the *mezuzah* come with anything else?" The wealthy man responded, "Yes it came with instructions inside. But since I was sure you knew how to use it, I threw it out." This man thought the beautiful covering was all that mattered. He didn't realize the value was the *klaf* with its beautiful words of Torah.

Don't just look at the silver covering; determine if the person's character is sterling.

There is a *midrash* of a woman who dresses a cat in an apron and hat and teaches it to serve. She invites company and the cat serves beautifully until a mouse comes along; then the cat acted like its natural self and chased the mouse. You can't change a person's basic nature easily. Don't get fooled by the external façade - find out the real nature of a person.

There was a woman who divorced a Congressman and married a garbage man. Her friends were shocked. She said, "A garbage man is what he does, not what he is." Judge people by their character; not by their title or wealth.

Don't judge a person's every word or analyze their every thought. Get a total feel for the person. My father used to say, "Don't wonder whether you can live with another person the rest of your life – no one will measure up. Go out. Each time you are together, decide if you like being with this person. Before you know it, you'll realize, 'I really enjoy being with this person. I just want to keep on being with him or her'. Take one day at a time. It adds up to a lifetime."

Everyone thinks they know who is good for whom, but it's not up to other people to say who is right for you. You must know what you want and decide if the person meets your needs. You may bring out qualities in him that others don't see.

Remember, everyone else disappears after the wedding. You are the only one who will live with the person. If you two were the only people in the world, and you didn't have to consider other people's opinions, would you want to be with this person? However, though you don't want to be influenced by friends who may subconsciously be jealous or have their own ulterior motives, you should recognize the sincere opinions about your potential spouse of family members and others you respect. Consider their opinions, although you may not necessarily accept them.

If a boy or girl isn't right for your friend, it doesn't mean s/he is not right for you. If all your friends say someone is great, it still doesn't mean he is right for you. If *everyone* says someone is wrong for you, it doesn't mean they are right. Look into each person for yourself and base your decision on your own instincts, not on your insecurities.

"Marriage is often a case of two people agreeing to change each other's habits."

It's important to love a person as they are. You can't count on changing someone. However, you can influence a person to grow if s/he is bright, flexible and wants to make you happy. You must also be flexible. You need not change your beliefs or ideals, but in life and marriage there are many areas that need working through; if you don't bend with the wind, you will break.

Getting a husband is like buying a house. You don't see it the way it is, but the way you think it's going to be when you get it remodeled.

Don't marry someone feeling you will remodel him, though people do grow and mature. However, don't only look at what a person is right now; look at his or her potential.

Rebbetzin Feinstein told an important story. Before she was engaged, she was concerned that she was taller than Rav Moshe. Her father said to her, "One day Rav Feinstein will be much taller than everyone." Height is not only measured in feet and inches.

Knowing how to judge a person's potential is crucial. Dina said, "When I met my husband he was serious, focusing on certain things. I knew if I could become one of those 'certain things' he'd be focused on me. So I worked at getting him to like me and now I am his main focus; he is a devoted husband."

It is essential to know what to look for in a spouse. Look for someone loving and compassionate, warm and understanding, sensitive and tuned in, honest and giving. It's nice to be with someone who shares your interests, appreciates your sense of humor and has a pleasant sense of humor which you enjoy. It is wonderful to share your life with someone who is bright, whom you respect and with whom you like talking and doing things. It is essential to be with someone who is at the same place religiously, and who wants what you want socially and economically. Find someone who shares and supports your goals and dreams.

The transition to married life is easier when you and your spouse come from similar backgrounds and have similar hopes for your life.

Look at the total composition of influences on a person. A person is comprised of many elements and influences such as:

Family: Are the members close, caring, well liked etc? How is the parent's relationship? How many members are in the family? Where does this person fall within the family? Who are the siblings and who did they marry? Is the family prominent or low keyed, showy or humble? Is there divorce or illness in the family? These are not necessarily a deterrent but all the ingredients have to be taken into account. How charitable are they? Do they have an open home? Perhaps some of these things may not matter to you, but you should be aware of them.

It is ideal to find a spouse compatible with your family. Your relationship with everyone around you is affected by whom you marry.

Yichus: People's origins should be taken into account. Again, this may be neither favorable nor unfavorable, but it should be considered in the equation. Polish, Hungarian, Sephardic, German, Russian, and American families have different habits, customs and styles.

Social and Economic Status: People need not marry someone within their own class, but it's important to be aware of the differences. A wealthy girl may not be comfortable married to a boy who can't treat her in the style she is accustomed to. This does not mean she can not adjust to having less, but it is an added challenge (and one, I believe, the Torah does not ask her to make.)

Religious Status: What is the level of religious observance? Is s/he *frum* from birth or a *baal teshuvah*? Is s/he involved in *kiruv*?

Personality: What type of personality does s/he have? Is s/he sweet and giving, or tough and self centered, sensitive or indifferent, relaxed or intense, optimistic or negative? Is s/he outgoing or introverted, quiet or loud, funny or bitingly sarcastic? Different qualities appeal to different people.

There are two types of people in the world: those who come into a room and say, "Here I am!" and those who come in and say, "Ah, there you are!"

A mate with a good heart helps everything. People don't tire of someone who is good to them and for them, unless he has no other appealing qualities, or the first person is too immature to appreciate him.

Stan was so nice and sweet someone worried whether he could be a strong leader of a family. Nice, sweet people can run a family with sweetness. Meet the person. Judge each person individually.

Determine if this person is truly ready for marriage and its responsibilities. You want a devoted person who cares about your needs and desires.

Look for a person who does *chessed* as part of his or her makeup, not because it's part of his agenda. Some people help their siblings with homework, help their parents with house chores, open doors for elderly women, give up their seats on a bus for another person who is standing, or volunteer at the hospital without thinking of it as a burden; it's a natural part of their being. Others go about their own self-centered lives, making a point to do *chessed* once a week; they are unconcerned about the three people they knock over while running to fulfill their *chessed* hour. Many people work on themselves to be more *chessed* conscious. Be the right kind of person and find the right kind of person.

Rebbetzin Alpert told me her Poppa (Rabbi Chaim Pinchas Scheinberg shlita) wanted in-laws who taught their children *Mesiras Nefesh*.

The argument you just won with your wife isn't over yet.

It is wise to choose a flexible person. You want a person with standards, opinions and convictions who can also understand and consider your feelings. It's a delicate mix of strength and caring, of sticking to your beliefs and being flexible and compromising.

Most people want someone who will be a best friend to them; someone who is able to be energetic and fun yet mature and responsible.

Attraction: It is not important to marry someone brilliant, handsome, gorgeous or super talented. It is important to marry someone you are attracted to, who is smart enough to meet your needs and whose looks appeal to you.

A happy, smiley disposition makes people appealing whether they are good looking or not.

Someone advised me not to marry someone who thinks his mother always looks perfect. You'll never be able to live up to her because he's not being realistic. On the other hand, there are boys who think their wives always look perfect. Find one of these.

Intellect: This includes his level of Torah learning, in addition to his secular learning and street smarts. My grandfather always told me, "A person is like a nail. If you stick a nail in the wrong place, you can always pull it out and place it somewhere else if the nail has a head. However, if the nail does not have a head, you can't pull it out, and it remains stuck there. A person must also have a good head on his shoulders so if he finds himself in the wrong place (the wrong career, the wrong location, the wrong school, etc.), he can pull himself out and do something else. But if he doesn't have a good head, he can't make the changes necessary to handle life." There is a lot of adjusting to do in life, particularly in a marriage.

One *shadchan* said an important quality to look for is *chachmas lev* (a smart, understanding heart).

Goals or ambitions: Is he a learner, earner or combination? A person's goals and dreams, his *hashkafah*, and his plans for the way he hopes to work, learn, live and raise a family must enter the equation.

Someone advised me, "Ask yourself if s/he is a *Baal(as) Aliyah*, someone always moving upward, trying to make more of him or herself." Is the person solid and does he use his time well?

Couples should share the same goals of raising and providing for their family. It's fine for each to succeed in the business world with the man entering finance and the woman practicing law, as long as they respect each other's personal goals and stay involved in the other's daily life. Often people focusing on their individual different goals, veer off, each going their own way.

Before a person is born, a heavenly voice declares, *"Bas Ploni LePloni"* ("the daughter of so-and-so to so-and-so"). Rabbi Matisyahu Salomon explains that each partner has the potential to enable the other to achieve the ultimate purpose for which s/he was created. In searching for a life partner focus on finding that person with whom one will be able to accomplish your predestined purpose.

The Entire Package: No one can tell you whom you will "click" with or to whom you will be attracted. The person who is right for you, can be comprised of different percentages of qualities.

Find the right percentage mix of qualities that appeal to you.

	Person A	Person B	Person C	Person D	Person E
Goals	10%	20%	8%	3%	2%
Religious outlook	10%	20%	30%	10%	5%
Personality	15%	5%	10%	10%	30%
Family	12%	5%	2%	20%	10%
Looks	10%	5%	20%	1%	11%
Caring and warmth	10%	8%	12%	40%	5%
Talent	8%	2%	2%	9%	2%
Intelligence	20%	35%	6%	1%	20%
Economic bracket	5%	0%	10%	6%	15%
	100%	100%	100%	100%	100%

"To judge a man's character by only one of its manifestations is like judging the sea by a jug full of its water."

Always focus on the total person. "My fiancé is losing his hair but he's so warm and sensitive." "He's not book smart but he has unbelievable street smarts." "She's never on time but when she does show up, it's always great to be with her." Don't ever fool yourself into thinking there's a person without some type of issue.

A girl and boy see each other and are attracted to one another. Do they talk? No; they go home and research the other one. If the boy is nice, sweet and smart, but not brilliant or well off, the girl may be unwilling to date him, unaware that his sweetness and warmth can compensate for the absence of these other qualities. His charm or drive may compensate for lack of wealth. His personality compensates for mediocre looks, etc.

There is no rule to determine who is right for you. If you're quiet, should you marry a quiet or loud person? If you are funny should you marry someone who is also funny or someone who appreciates your sense of humor? If you're aggressive should you marry someone laid back or another aggressive person? There is no right answer. Opposites attract or aren't attracted. Each person must decide which characteristics appeal to him or her.

I want a husband who is decent, G-d fearing, well educated, smart, sincere, respectful, treats me as an equal, is healthy, and has the same interests in life as me. Now I don't think that's too much to ask of a billionaire, do you?

A common misconception is thinking the person you marry must fulfill your *every* need. This is not true. S/he does not take the place of everyone else in your life. Your spouse is an addition - an important addition - but an addition, not a replacement. If your husband doesn't make you laugh all the time but your brother is very funny, you can still call your brother for a good laugh. If your wife doesn't love to play sports with you, you can still play with your father. However it is crucial that you determine which of your needs your husband or wife must meet.

Marry someone who loves and appreciates what and who you are. It is better to marry less of a person who appreciates you more, than more of a person who appreciates you less.

People can be defined by their bad habits. Does he drive too fast and out of control? Does he scream at other people on the road? Would you want him to be the person driving you around for the rest of your life? Does he smoke or drink too much? Even at *simchos* a person should not drink too much, especially if he is driving home. Is she impatient? Is he quick tempered? Does she get furious if I show up a few minutes late? Is he a sore loser? Does she cheat?

A woman bought a parrot. The parrot was unhappy so the woman returned to the pet store and told the salesman the parrot was unhappy. The salesman said, "Did you try buying the parrot a swing? He'll go on the swing and that will make him happy." She bought the swing but the bird was still unhappy. She returned to the pet shop. "Did you try buying the parrot a ladder?" asked the salesman. "The bird will climb the ladder and swing on the swing and then the parrot will be happy." The woman bought the ladder, but the bird was still unhappy. This time the salesman asked whether the woman had bought the parrot a bell. He said, "The parrot will climb the ladder, swing on the swing and ring the bell, then it will be happy." So the woman bought the bell. The next day the woman returned to the pet store and angrily told the salesman that her parrot had died. The salesman said, "Did the parrot say anything before he died?" "Oh yes," said the woman, "the parrot said, 'Doesn't that store sell any bird food?' "

It is essential to know and prioritize your needs. If a person has a lot of great qualities but they aren't the ones that make you happy, they are worthless.

On a man's fiftieth anniversary, he burst out crying. Someone inquired why he was crying. He said, "If I had killed my wife fifty years ago, by now I'd be out of prison."

Please G-d, you will live a long time with the person you marry, so be sure to choose the person who appeals to you and is right for you for a life sentence, not just for the short term.

A person can marry different types of people. The direction your life takes has a lot to do with whom you marry. A wife can develop or stifle her husband's potential and vice versa. She can encourage her spouse, making him better, or discourage him, making him bitter. A spouse can give an insecure person confidence. He can give you courage and encouragement; she can back you up and be on your team. He can hinder and frustrate you, making you lose self esteem; she can continually question you, making you feel more alone.

Some people are attracted to quiet people, some to people who are outgoing, some to people with confidence. Others are attracted by warmth or a good sense of humor. Still others are attracted to someone who is non-judgmental, or easy going, or to someone controlling or organized. People's choices are affected by their needs, desires, insecurities, dreams, the other person's potential, what they have heard about the other person, and by what they perceive.

Some people choose what they lack; that is where opposites attract. A shy person may choose an aggressive person because they complement each other. Other people are attracted to someone just like themselves. Someone involved in athletics may be attracted to someone who shares this interest.

Be open-minded, understanding your own needs, and the other person's ability to meet those needs. Don't decide you can live without certain needs being met. Don't find excuses for the other person. Be smart. Don't fool the other person and don't fool yourself. Of course, make sure your needs are realistic.

Happiness is the conviction that we are loved for in spite of ourselves.

How do you feel when you are around this person? S/he may be special, but do you feel special around him? Are you in his shadow, or an individual? You may like him but do you like yourself when you are with him? Does he make you feel good about yourself? He may be cute, but do you feel cute when you are with him? She may be smart, but do you feel smart around her? She may be great but do you feel great around her?

One of the most important elements in a relationship is feeling comfortable and being able to act yourself when you're with that person. You must feel s/he values your opinion and appreciates your special qualities such as your sense of humor, your intuition, your great patience, or your ability to learn, etc. You want someone who knows and likes the real you.

The right choice shapes the rest of your life, as well as your development into a wife, husband, friend, daughter, son, community worker, etc. A person with a spouse who encourages and supports him becomes better in *every* aspect of life.

A nice spouse makes you nice. A mean spouse makes you frustrated, angry, insecure and unsure of yourself. Don't marry someone who's hung up on himself; marry someone who knows how to love, be sacrificing, be supportive, and put you first. If both people put the other's needs first, both will like each other and themselves, and both will blossom and thrive.

Some people, who seemed secure when they were single, seem nervous, insecure and stagnant when they are married. Others, who seemed insecure while single, seem sure of themselves, able to move forward and accomplish after marriage. It's the spouse who can help build you up or break you down.

A girl's husband often becomes her mirror. She sees herself through his eyes. A girl can become anorexic because their husbands make them feel fat, though they are very thin. I once met a girl who stayed thin. She said, "It's because my husband cares." I thought, "That's so nice. How lucky she is," until she added, "He'd kill me if I gained an ounce." Then I realized that she had seemed confident about her figure, but was really very nervous and insecure about it. She got divorced soon after this conversation.

Larry was engaged to a gorgeous girl. He thought she looked fine, but not as exceptionally pretty as others thought. She will need lots of self confidence because he won't make her feel beautiful. On the other hand, I know a heavy girl whose husband thinks she's gorgeous. She always feels beautiful and confident.

Follow your instincts. Don't ignore them or push them aside. Don't make excuses. Don't think you can live with, or change the things that bother you. Perhaps you can, but before you commit to marriage, test your theory. Give it some time, going through different situations. Determine if the person will change or if you can tolerate the things that bother you. No one is perfect, but different people tolerate different things.

Girls may chase and get the boy they worship, but when the thrill of having snagged him wears off, they feel something is lacking. Instead of feeling a sense of delight, they feel insecure and inadequate. Busy trying to impress and meet the other person's needs, they didn't take the time to discover whether the other person was right for them or met their needs.

Murray was popular and could have had any girl he chose. He married Anne whom he believed was playing hard to get by acting cold and indifferent. Taking on the challenge, he was thrilled to capture Anne's heart. After the marriage, Murray discovered that Anne hadn't been acting cold and standoffish in order to appeal to him; rather this was her true personality. Now he is married to a cold, tough woman. Be sure to see a person for what he is, not for the challenge he poses or what you would like him to be.

My wife and I have a perfect understanding. I don't try to run her life and I don't try to run mine.

Joel married a girl because he loved how she related to elderly people. Later, he discovered she was only comfortable around old people and quite awkward with everyone else. Shirley was thrilled her boyfriend loved to spend time only with her. It never occurred to her that he was anti-social. Once again, avoid this by spending time with the person in as many different situations as possible.

You are picking a partner, so it must be someone with common goals, dreams and visions. You will share the good times, but need someone to lean on in the hard times. Lots of issues develop throughout life. Even the most compatible couples will deal with issues: Should we be strict or lenient with the kids? Should we stay in a smaller house where it's crowded, or move to a more spacious home and have financial pressure? Should we go to your relatives who aren't feeling well, or my relatives who haven't seen us in some time? Can you make these decisions before you are married? Can you make a list of the potential problems that might arise, seeing if you can agree on the solutions? No, but you can spend more quality time together. Time is the best answer. Spend enough time together to truly know the person. Evaluate how he handles different situations, and notice his potential for compromise. Make sure you communicate well, talking openly, honestly, and candidly. Your answers should be what you want to say, not what he wants to hear. His answers should not be molded in order to score points, rather they must reflect what he feels and how he plans to live. Get to know a person's true character. You can't imagine all the challenges life will hand you, but if you know each other well enough, you can deduce how s/he will react in other situations.

Nothing beats love at first sight except for love with insight.

Be aware that people are nervous on dates. Issac was pulling a door that said push, and Wendy thought, "What is with this boy?" Then she realized he was just nervous. Eventually Issac became more comfortable and Wendy married him.

My grandfather used to say, "Don't overestimate yourself, don't underestimate the other person." The reverse holds true too. Don't overestimate the other person and don't underestimate yourself. Try to judge the other person fairly, also analyzing his or her effect on you. An outgoing person may be great for one person, but stunt another. A quiet person may appeal to one person and frustrate another. Some people need continuous love. Some people need to be continuously challenged. Some people need a mixture. Figure out what is best for you.

Be aware that people's positive traits can have a negative side, and vice versa. An aggressive person may do well in business but is often hard to live with. A soft, quiet person may be easy to live with, but may not do well in business. Know your needs. Do you need an attentive person, do you need someone who will give you a financially secure life, or do you need a combination of both qualities (which is hard to find).

Even the right person will have things about them that bother you. Some things can be changed, some tolerated, some ignored or over looked, and some will disturb you all your life but you accept it as part of the package. You may spend your marriage hopelessly trying to change one of your spouse's habits – an annoying laugh, a sarcastic attitude, a tendency to be late, a quick temper, sloppiness, thriftiness, etc. But, hopefully s/he has plenty of qualities that compensate for the one or two that annoy you. The key is knowing what you can tolerate. What bothers one person may not bother the next and people have different tolerance levels for different things.

One Rabbi keeps a list of the things he loves about his wife; every time she does something special he records it. When she does something that annoys him, he glances at his list and remembers why he loves her.

One person may be thrilled with an easy going, soft spoken spouse, while another may not have the patience for "a pushover". Someone may be married to a loud, outgoing person while others feel s/he is self-centered and needs too much attention. Marry what appeals to you, not for the moment, but for the long run. A challenging boy was exciting to pursue and acquire, but not something I wanted for a lifetime.

A man who has imperfections is just about as perfect as anyone can be.

Define what bothers you and see if you can handle it for a lifetime. Is it worth giving up a wonderful boy or girl because s/he is always late, or sloppy, or finicky, etc.? However is it worth giving up someone who seems great, is good looking, learned, bright, successful and charming, yet sometimes loses control, acts mean, or belittles or embarrasses you in public. What if she can be unreasonable at times or he's unfeeling or, G-d forbid, violent? I believe it is worth giving up a "great" person if s/he has any mean hurtful qualities that are out of control.

Shimi dated two girls - my close friend Freeda and my sister's friend - seriously. Telling Freeda he'd be out of town for the weekend, Shimi would date my sister's friend. Because this happened quite a few times, I told Freeda he was lying to her. But Freeda refused to see this, perhaps because Shimi was in medical school and really handsome. Once, Shimi meanly accused Freeda of a lack of insight at a social event. However, eventually he broke up with the other girl, choosing Freeda. Freeda become the lucky winner of a lying, cheating and conniving boy, whom she married and later divorced. She had been busy pursuing him, too caught up in his credentials to see what he really was. She ignored the signs, making excuses for his bad behavior.

If a boy or girl has bad qualities don't defend him by saying, "He's different with me." Is he? Remember you can fool some of the people…he may be putting his best foot forward for you. Lisa dated some one who lied to her, making her feel insecure. He continually asked things like, "Why didn't you want to go to the concert last night?" or "Why didn't you show up at the party last night? I was waiting for you." When Lisa explained that he never mentioned these things to her, he'd answer, "Of course I asked you." He convinced Lisa that she wasn't listening to him, but he actually never told her about these events because he enjoyed his freedom. Rather than being upfront with Lisa, he made her feel frustrated with herself. Why marry someone who manipulates people like that?

"Wisdom is the power to put our time and our knowledge to proper use." *(Thomas Watson)*

Don't only make sure a boy is a good learner. There is no guarantee that good learners will be good doers. The idea is to incorporate what you learn into your daily living. Torah should help you learn caring, humility, modesty, compassion, and generosity, developing a person to be a better son, husband, father, and human being.

"You can give without loving, but you can't love without giving."

If you ask someone what type of husband he hopes to be, one boy might answer, "The most important thing is my learning. My learning must always come first," while another might say, "I always want to learn, but if my wife needs my help, I'll be there for her." Both boys are learning, but one is putting his learning into actions.

I have heard people complain that some *Yeshivos* turn out great *Talmidei Chachamim*, but not great husbands. *Chassan* (husbanding) classes are helpful, but schools should be encouraged to teach boys how to treat people, particularly their wives, earlier.

Examine a person's *midos* more than his philosophy. Don't only check if a boy is wearing a hat; check what's under the hat. Is he a *mentch*? A *Rebbetzin* told me that *midos* are a *yerushah*. One inherits one's *midos* just like one does the color of one's eyes. Observe the *midos* of the family.

Consider what a person is today and his growth potential. If a person has a history of which he is not proud, but has improved and made something of himself, and has matured and grown in Torah and *midos*, give him credit and accept him for what he has become.

Michael was a bit of a rebel in high-school but grew into an outstanding young man steeped in learning and pursuing a fine career. Rivka refused to date him saying she had known him in high-school. Rivka focused solely on his past and not on the outstanding individual he had become. Chana married him and has a husband who would make anyone proud.

"A rich man is nothing but a poor man with money"
(W.C. Fields)

Don't marry for money. It's cheaper to borrow it. Money doesn't buy happiness. Unfortunately, some people foolishly put money as a priority.

One girl only wanted to marry a lawyer. She dated an unrefined boy and didn't take notice, because he was a lawyer. When I introduced her to someone who was not yet a professional, she said, "He seems nice but is he fine?" I realized she could not see beyond the title.

Don't judge a man by the clothes he wears. G-d made one; the tailor made the other.

"Don't judge a book by its cover." Of course, you must be attracted to a person's outside, but you will live with his inside. Don't typecast people. Look within each individual.

People define "great" differently. I told someone a certain girl was great. She said, "I always thought 'great' meant warm, mushy and loving." I said, "That's also true and this girl isn't necessarily those things. Yet she is still 'great' because she's bright, pretty, sharp, good natured, and aggressive, with a solid, prestigious, family. All her siblings married spouses who don't need warm, mushy people." Would I prefer warmth? The perfect girl for my son would ooze warmth, but I recognize that many people who don't have this quality are considered a "great" catch, and are indeed great for the right person. This holds true for lots of qualities.

My wife asked me if I want a large family. I told her I did, so she sent for hers!

Children learn what they see in their home. How they translate what they see determines the kind of person and spouse they will be. A *baal teshuva* may see beautiful *midos* in his home and grow in *halachik* commitment on his own.

A brilliant man travels to Russia to make a speech. At the conclusion, he is very disappointed with his light applause. The next speaker, a Russian, elicits more applause each minute. The original speaker doesn't understand the speech but claps out of politeness. A third man turns to him and says, "It's not nice to applaud." The first speaker says, "Why not?" The man says, "Because he is translating your speech." It is best to see how children translate what they have learned from their parents.

What if a girl or boy has a wonderful reputation, but either his parents are divorced, or she has no *yichus,* or there was an unfortunate scandal in the family, or the family is impoverished? Everyone has baggage. Judge a person *Lekaf Zechus*, by getting to know him personally.

The majority of children from broken marriages don't want their children hurt as they were, and therefore make good spouses, working at their own marriages. Unfortunately, some children of divorced parents have never seen couples work through difficult situations; that is why statistics show children from divorced families have a higher divorce rate.

Determine the kind of parents this individual has, as you would in any other *shidduch.* Are they each good people who were merely incompatible? What is the relationship between the divorced parents and their relationship to their children and new spouses and families?

It may be complicated to involve yourself with someone from divorced parents, but s/he may be worth it. S/he may have matured earlier. He may understand life's pressures. She may have learned greater independence. He may have learned to be more responsible and sensitive. On the other hand, he can be angrier, less tolerant or less in need of love. You must consider how the divorce affected and continues to affect this person, but realize that the effects can be positive.

My daughter dated a couple of boys from divorced parents and each one was impressive. People should research the person, and give him or her a fair chance.

By the time I decided to consider a boy whose parents were divorced for my daughter, the *shadchan* said, "Don't bother feeling sorry for him; he's already engaged." I quickly learned that a terrific boy, even with divorced parents, is still in demand.

Judge people from homes where the parents are separated, like other people. Life and its circumstances affect everyone in different ways. See how this person was affected.

Consider how long a *baal teshuva* has been studying, how advanced he is, and how committed he is. When did he become a *baal teshuva*? Is his family supportive or negative? Is there any feeling for Judaism in the family? Is intermarriage practiced and accepted? What are the family's values like? Are they in sync with your own values? How solid is he? *Baalei teshuva* may swing back or become too fanatic for you. You must be certain they are heading where you plan on being.

On the other hand, *baalei teshuva* often work on improving themselves. They are idealistic and often quite bright, accepting *Hashem* on an intellectual level. They usually appreciate things FFBs (frum from birth) take for granted. They enjoy taking on *mitzvos*. They often love and appreciate the warmth of *Rabbis* and their families.

Again, look at the individual. Some *baalei teshuvah* are searching, open minded and work on their *midos* and learning. Others are closed minded and rigid, with the strong influences of their background continually affecting their growth.

Don't categorize a person. Being a *baal teshuvah* is only one of a person's characteristics; is she kind, is he fine, is he nice? That is what truly matters. My son-in-law is a *baal teshuvah*. Everyone should grow in Torah and *Mitzvos* with his devotion and enthusiasm.

Widows, people with children, and people with special problems can be wonderful candidates as spouses, but each has to be judged individually. When considering taking on this kind of a relationship, decide whether you can handle the situation and the responsibilities that accompany this union.

Some individuals date for a very long time or go out with too many people without making a commitment. They develop a reputation of being either a tease or burnt out. It can be explained away once or even twice, but sooner or later you are branded. Eventually most people find what they are looking for, but it can be hard to date someone like this.

Some families seem to have children who don't get married. They date but for various reasons don't commit. If you come from such a family, push yourself to overcome what ever is standing in your way of commitment.

People from particular areas may have certain similarities and they are often judged by their hometown. New Yorkers are often faster paced, where as out-of-towners are softer and less aggressive. Brooklyn, Queens, Long Island, Monsey or New Jersey have their own style. Even neighborhoods or groups within these communities seem to produce different personality types. Right-wing out-of-towners are often more worldly than those brought up in New York. Girls from Cleveland or Seattle may be more likely to move away from their families, realizing there is a limited Jewish population where they live and expecting to move wherever their husband is living. California girls often want to return to their homes and beautiful weather. Consider where the person comes from, whether s/he fits the norm for that community and whether this interests you. My son said people often sing the praises of out-or-town girls, yet hesitate to let their children date them for fear they will move near their families.

Remember though, to judge each person for himself, considering background, character and expectations.

Relationship Advice: Criticism breaks down a relationship. A spoon full of sugar makes the medicine go down. Compliment while you correct.

Of all human passions love is the strongest, for it attacks the head, the heart and the senses simultaneously.

APPEARANCES - ATTRACTION

I married her for her looks, but not the ones she's been giving me lately!

People often accuse singles of superficiality when they mention attractiveness, but this is unfair because the request is realistic. However, "attractive" is different for each person. Even a gorgeous girl may not be attractive to someone who finds her cold or distant looking, or who feels she is too tall or too thin. People may find a beautiful smile or a twinkling eye an attraction. Some boys love thin girls with a plain face, while others love a pretty face and are not focused on weight. It is true that looks are in the eyes of the beholder.

Don't fool yourself. You don't need a great looking spouse but you must be attracted to him.

Looks include facial features, height, weight, build, hair color, complexion and the amount and length of one's hair. Different combinations of these features cause a person to be beautiful, cute, handsome, pleasant, nice looking, mediocre or unattractive to another individual.

But a person's looks are only one of the many ingredients that account for attraction. People are attracted to a warm and bubbly personality; to someone with a friendly and caring disposition or an easygoing and charming demeanor; to someone learned, intelligent, interesting or knowledgeable; to someone shy and modest, or to someone outgoing and charismatic. These characteristics shine through a person's face.

A bright, sensitive, intuitive, athletic or talented person may cause others to be attracted to him or her despite his physical features. A boy sitting in the center of a crowd, playing guitar and singing melodiously can impress you no matter what he looks like. A person who smiles warmly at you, offering to help with your heavy packages may appeal to you even if his features are not impressive.

Some individuals enjoy a challenge and are drawn to someone who seems hard to get. Some people exude so much confidence no one realizes their features are plain. They think highly of themselves so others think highly of them also. A person's demeanor or the way he carries himself contributes to his total appearance. (Discussed in greater depth in the chapter "The Person.")

I'm tired of this nonsense about beauty being only skin deep. That's deep enough. What do you want - an adorable pancreas? *(Jean Kerr)*

A person might say he wants a blonde, fair skinned spouse, yet fall for a dark, black haired spouse and vice versa. Sometimes people give me ridiculous specifics. A boy might say, "I want a girl around five foot three, with blue eyes, dark hair, and long legs who is a size six." Six months later he's engaged to a girl five foot eight, who wears a size fourteen, with red hair and brown eyes. He looks overjoyed because he has found exactly what he wanted. Or he may take out a girl who is four foot ten, with mediocre features and a charming smile, and be walking on cloud nine since he found the girl of his dreams. (See chapter "You Never Know.")

I've repeated this often and the message still remains true: Meet and judge a person for yourself. What you hear about his or her personality, *midos*, goals etc. must first appeal to you; the reports about the individual's looks or personality should not turn you off.

One thing you can be sure of – there will always be more people going on a diet tomorrow than those on a diet today.

During this time period every person should look the best they can. The girl or boy should be in shape, wear the most flattering clothing, and find the best hair cut, and girls should wear appealing makeup.

People may agree that boys should not refuse to date a heavier girl; nevertheless, heavier girls do have a harder time getting dates. People ask, "Is she thin?" as if nothing else matters. One mother handed me a card with her daughter's name and wrote on it, "size six".

The Jewish community has a horrific problem, since many girls - and even boys - are anorexic and/ or bulimic. Whereas one out of five hundred women in the U.S.A. is anorexic, some statistics maintain that one out of fifty women in Orthodox Jewish circles deal with this issue. Anorexia can have devastating medical consequences such as sterility and, in extreme cases, death.

One cause is the pressure of the *shidduch* system. Although parents should encourage children to stay in shape, do not pressure daughters to be overly weight conscious, which can cause anorexia. Men should not demand emaciated girls, which is very unhealthy.

The pressure can have a negative affect because if a boy hears that a girl is anorexic or bulimic, he will refuse to date her.

"I sent my wife to a diet farm. She lost half her weight in two weeks."
"How much longer do you want her to stay?"
"Two weeks."

Unfortunately, weight is given too much "weight" in this system. Overweight girls have a tough time dating in the *shidduch* system where the decision to date someone is based on what you heard about the person, rather than meeting someone and liking him despite his size. Unfairly, heavy boys often refuse to date heavy girls. Even heavy boys are often in demand, and they feel they can get thin girls.

Now boys want a girl to be a size two. Truthfully, lots of size twelve and size fourteen girls have great figures and are attractive. Certainly they may have great eyes, great personalities, a great sense of humor, or a great head. These characteristics are just as important.

Of course, some boys prefer *"zaftig"* girls (with a little meat on their bones) and aren't attracted to overly thin girls.

Very heavy parents can reflect poorly on the girl. Parents also must make a good impression, since most people believe children follow in their parent's footsteps.

Don't consider looks alone. The best-looking boys may lose their hair early and develop pot-bellies. Some of the prettiest girls lose their figures and develop double chins.

If you like the person but don't feel an attraction, don't reject him out of hand. Perhaps you can sensitively encourage him to improve his looks. What if she got lenses or changed her hair style? What if he lost weight, bought new glasses, grew his hair, trimmed his beard or fixed his teeth? Someone encouraged a great boy to have a nose job and his ears pinned back; now she finds him nice looking and a terrific husband.

Personal taste does matter. Doni said he didn't care about looks. Then he was set up with someone extremely unattractive. He married the next pretty girl he was *rhed*.

Do you want someone good looking because you are attracted to him, or to impress your friends? It is not necessary to impress others. It does nothing for you and can cause jealousy in others. But if you want someone who makes your heart skip when he smiles at you, why shouldn't you have it?

Rafi was a boy with excellent values. He was disappointed in himself when he realized he wanted a pretty girl, feeling he was being superficial. Was he choosing looks over *midos?* He wasn't. He wanted a girl who was beautiful on the inside, but at the same time he needed to be attracted to her.

Marvin took a girl to a dimly lit restaurant on the first date. He insisted on going to a well-lit restaurant or on being seated near a window for the second date, to determine whether or not he was attracted to her.

Everyone deserves someone who appeals to them. One bright *Rebbetzin* wisely tells people her children are looking for someone "aesthetically compatible".

Beauty is in the eyes of the beholder. One brother with three gorgeous sisters said his girlfriend Ildy was better looking than any of them. Ildy was heavy and not very good-looking, but she was a great girl, which made her seem pretty. A person's insides, her or his warmth, goodness, or sweetness shines through and affects her appearance.

Jason told his parents the girl he was dating looked okay. Their jaws dropped when they met her because she was stunning! Jason wanted to marry her because of the total package, and hadn't even realized she was so beautiful.

Although looks are subjective, some people are universally considered good looking or not good looking. Whenever people lectured me about not judging looks, it usually meant the girl's positive characteristic was not her looks. Of course, she will still appeal to others because of different qualities that she possesses.

He took my glasses off and said, "Without your glasses, why, you're beautiful."
I said, "Without my glasses, you're not half bad either." *(Kit Hollerbach)*

In a story "When Harry Met Sally" Harry tells his friend that Sally is smart. The other boy says, "So you're trying to say she's not good looking." Harry answers, "No, she's smart and good looking." His friend says, "If she's really good looking, you wouldn't have said she's smart; you would have said she's good looking." Sally, of course was both. Saying a person is smart doesn't mean they aren't good looking, or vice versa. Saying someone is charming, does not mean he isn't smart or good looking. Perhaps his special charm is a most unique quality.

You can ask other people their opinion, if someone says he doesn't know about the person's looks. But keep in mind that everyone has different taste.

Get to know the person as a whole rather than focusing only on his looks. But, you must be attracted to, as well as attractive for your spouse.

The average girl would rather have beauty than brains because the average boy can see better than he can think.

Someone asked if my son would mind being fixed up with a gorgeous girl. I thought the question was ridiculous until I realized that it makes some people insecure; they are afraid the girl will focus on herself, take the limelight or be too demanding. Being too pretty can be a problem. Girls also may not want an unattractive man, but are nervous about extremely good looks. As always, judge each person for his or herself.

How important is height? This is up to the individual. I know tall girls married to short boys and tall boys married to tiny girls. Some people obsess about height, but most people think it is just another part of the whole person. Girls will be lucky to get some short boys with outrageous personalities. Some super tall girls are so warm and good- natured that a boy would be blessed to marry them. People from very short or very tall family are usually more concerned with height, worried their offspring will be either extremely short or extremely tall. There is nothing wrong with a girl marrying a boy shorter than her as long as she looks up to him, and there is nothing wrong with a boy marrying a girl taller than him as long as she doesn't look down on him.

Sherri was set up with a very short boy. She busily debated whether she could overlook his height and keep dating him. Meanwhile, he called the *shadchan* to say he was not interested in seeing Sherri again.

People are judged by their appearances. Dress is an important part of that. Flattering clothing can make you look attractive despite your features. Your dress should reflect the type of person you are. Those who dress in designer clothing may appeal to some people while making others uncomfortable. A person's clothing usually says something about the person's personality, social status or even aspirations.

Don't be forced to continue dating someone if you truly dislike a lot about his appearance, chin, teeth, jaw, nose, hair or overall build. People may say the attraction will come. Make sure it is there before you commit, otherwise, you may be frustrated for life.

However, don't let looks mean everything. *Sheker hachayn v'hevel hayofi* (beauty can be deceiving). Don't let someone's good looks keep you from seeing his real personality. Don't let superficiality keep you from seeing his real essence. Have a discerning eye.

Do you know the best way for a boy to impress a girl at the gym? Do pull-ups! Pull up in a Convertible, pull up in a Rolls Royce, pull up in a Cadillac...

AFTER THE DATE

A wife said to her husband, "Let's not stay home all the time. Let's go out three times a week."

The husband said, "Good idea. You go out Monday, Wednesday and Friday, I'll go out Sunday, Tuesday and Thursday."

After the date, both girl and boy should call the *shadchan*. Once in a while, the couple may decide to go out again between themselves, but it is still proper to call the *shadchan*, informing her that it went well, and that they will be speaking to one another directly.

People can use a *shadchan* as long as they feel it is necessary. Some people call the *shadchan* even after the fourth or fifth date. Others keep the *shadchan* involved for longer periods of time.

Call the *shadchan* as soon as possible. If they both liked each other, the *shadchan* will arrange with the boy to call again and then let the girl know when that will be. A *shadchan* makes lots of calls and negotiations, but the feeling is exhilarating if a *shidduch* works out.

If you do not want to go out again, or refuse to meet someone for the first time, say this in a manner that reflects kindly on both parties. State the positives and then explain that there was no chemistry or that it didn't click. Rather than telling the *shadchan* the girl was boring, thank her and say, "I just felt she wasn't for me."

A few kind words take only seconds to say, but their echoes can go on for years.

On the other hand, one boy called me after each date and raved about the girl, making me think, "this is it", until he'd add, "The only thing is…" That meant: "Who else do you have for me?"

If you are unsure but think there may be a possibility of a *shidduch* working out, explain what bothered you to the *shadchan*. Sometimes the *shadchan* can straighten it out. A girl went out with a boy who wore his hat all night. He did so because she dressed formally, but she dressed formally because she knew he was coming in a hat and suit. Each felt uncomfortable about the other's dress and therefore felt stiff and uptight. A *shadchan* can explain to the boy that the girl was advised to dress up, likewise telling the girl the boy was advised to wear a hat all night.

The common phrases to refuse to see someone again are, "It didn't work out," "It's not for me," or "It's not *shayach*," "It's not *nogayah*."

Judge every person you date *L'kaf Zechus* . If a girl seems irritable, perhaps she heard some bad news that day. If a boy seems to be rushing the date, perhaps he must get home to study.

A Rabbi fixed Shaindy up with Ari, whom he considered one of his top boys. Ari asked Shaindy to go out on Sunday. Shaindy explained that she had prior obligations that could not be pushed off on Sunday and wondered if they might go out a different day. However Ari answered that he had been in *aveilus* and had not been out for a year, so he was anxious to begin. Foolishly, Shaindy agreed to a Sunday date, but she was extremely tired. When Ari arrived she asked if they might go out locally. Ari wanted to go to Manhattan. Shaindy apologized for her fatigue, reminding Ari of her long day. Despite this, Ari kept her out for hours until, overcome with exhaustion, Shaindy momentarily dozed off. She was embarrassed. He was angry and reported to his Rabbi that Shaindy had fallen asleep. Shouldn't Ari have judged her *L'kaf Zechus*? Shaindy tried to understand his desire to enjoy a night out after his long period of *aveilus*. Ari should have understood that she'd had an extremely long day.

At the conclusion of the trial the judge asked the foreman if the jury had reached a verdict. "Your honor," answered the Jewish foreman, "we the jury have decided we should not mix in."

When one of the parties is not interested, the *shadchan* is challenged. The *shadchan* must be sensitive, speaking tactfully and delicately. If the boy is uninterested in the girl, the *shadchan* should mention that the boy is not interested, before the girl can say she is interested, allowing the girl to save face. She can also say, "I too, was not really interested."

The *shadchan* must let the person down easily, by saying something like, "He thought you were very nice; just not for him." That's sufficient. However, without being nosey or pushy, a *shadchan* can try to make things work. If the boy says, "I didn't like her; she was loud," the *shadchan* can say, "I know she really isn't loud, she was probably just nervous, why don't you try again?" and then discuss that issue with the girl. If the boy says, "I was not attracted to her at all," the *shadchan* can encourage the boy to try again. Sometimes attraction comes when you get to know someone, but often, the *shadchan* cannot make a *shidduch* work without attraction. But he can set up the person more appropriately the next time.

Always thank the person who fixed you up whether or not the date went well. Don't criticize *shadchanim* or talk badly of them, or people will be afraid to fix you up with *shidduchim*. The most unlikely *shidduchim* work, while people who seem perfect for each other don't click. (See chapter "You Never Know.") Show appreciation and *Hakaras Hatov* if someone *rheds* you *shidduchim*.

Jot down your thoughts after each date to develop a sense of what is important to you. Each date is a learning experience.

My son was about seven when he looked into our wedding album and said, "Pop, are these pictures of the day Mom came to work for us?"

BREAKING UP

Eve said to the serpent, "You know I could go for a bite to eat, but I don't know you from Adam." *(Red Buttons)*

An old song by Neil Sedaka is called, "Breaking Up Is Hard to Do". Never were truer words spoken. There is an indescribable emptiness that often accompanies breaking up.

I once broke up with a boy I didn't like. Afterwards I burst into tears, depressed because I should have given him another chance. I felt empty, sad and upset that I had to start all over. At least he was company. In my depression I told him we should try again. He was thrilled. As soon as I saw him again, I thought, "What did I do? This boy gets on my nerves." Of course I stopped seeing him after that.

It taught me that even someone who is not for you fills a void in your life. That's why people find it hard to stop dating someone even when the person isn't for them. People make excuses for the other person or are blind to certain things, because having no one and starting over is hard. Imagine, *Kal Vachomer* how hard it is to break up with someone you like and admire but just isn't for you. People often drag relationships for this reason. Having invested so much time and energy in it, they hate to give it up. But dating must lead to marriage or it is a waste of valuable time. Marriage is hopefully for life.

Invest enough time to get to know someone well, but walk away and move on if the person is not what you want. Don't trade time for possibilities.

If you aren't sure, go out until you are certain one way or the other. Though some people may say that's unfair to the other person, if he likes you, you are giving him another opportunity to get you to like him. Give honest feedback to the person himself or the *shadchan* so the person is not shocked if you do break up.

This is also true if, after you've stopped seeing someone, you reconsider. If the other person is willing to go out with you again, go for it! It's giving you another chance to see if you like the person and it's giving him another chance to make you like him.

A *shadchan* is handy in a break up situation, acting as the messenger and of course being diplomatic. By immediately saying the person no longer wants to continue, the interested party can save face by saying something like, "I too was losing interest."

Whether through the *shadchan* or directly you break up with another person, be tactful and sensitive to the other person's feelings. First mention that you appreciated his virtues (restoring a person's pride and some semblance of confidence) then add that you don't see any future to this relationship.

If you have already eliminated the *shadchan*, you owe the girl or boy some explanation, which you should deliver yourself. It should not be anything specific or hurtful. Say things like: "I don't feel we are right for each other" or "Though you are terrific, we have different life goals, *hashkafos* or different ideas of how we want to live our lives, or "I don't feel what I should be feeling."

Some people believe it is courteous to break up in person on a date. I disagree. To make a person get dressed up and get their hopes up, just to be told the relationship is over, seems cruel. If you are no longer interested, a phone call will suffice. It's no *mitzvah* to hurt a person. It is an emotional time and people feel vulnerable, so treat them delicately.

If you are not certain you want to break up, yet feel things are not progressing as they should, discuss the idea of breaking off the relationship on a date, seeing how the other person responds. In this case, a face-to-face discussion lets you see one another's emotions, and may help you decide one way or the other.

If you decide s/he is not right for you during a date, continue to be courteous. If you are not using a *shadchan* anymore, break up at the end of the date, at the door. Otherwise you are both forced to still spend time together during the ride home.

Someone broke up with a girl during the date, explaining that they weren't for each other. He said it was awkward and uncomfortable, but after he broke up with her, he was so much more relaxed, the rest of the date was actually the best time he ever spent with her. But he added, "I would never do that again."

Break up on amicable terms, leaving the person with a good feeling about you. Courteously say something like "I enjoyed the time we spent together but..."or "You have a wonderful sense of humor or a terrific personality but..."

It is kind to suggest fixing the person up with a friend. It is even nicer to follow up and find someone else for the person to date.

It is a disservice to yourself and the other person to continue dating someone only because you don't want to hurt him by breaking it off. Once it is determined that s/he is not right for you, s/he may get more emotionally involved if you stretch it out. It drains both of you.

Yudi tortured himself for four days about breaking up with a certain girl whom he had dated three times. He asked all his friends whether he should do it in person or over the phone and what he should say. He finally called her and said, "I think you are a great girl but." She said, "It was a communication problem, right?" Yudi answered, "Right." She politely said, "Okay." He said he'd keep his eyes open for a good boy for her. After days of worry, Yudi broke up in less than thirty seconds.

Barry told Sandra that he was breaking up with her. Sandra told him he wasn't. Barry insisted he was. Sandra persisted in insisting he wasn't. I suppose Sandra was right because I attended their wedding.

Murray told Rita he felt they were not right for one another. Rita furiously demanded to know how he came to this conclusion on his own, without discussing it with her. She added that no one ever broke up with her, and if he was so inconsiderate he should not bother to phone her again. Some people do not make it easy for you to break up with them.

Though it is painful when someone breaks up with you, take the attitude: I'm still terrific. It's his or her loss.

"Closure." Someone asked what people did before they invented this word. Everyone asks for it. Everyone deserves it. If you are not interested in a person, don't keep them hanging on and hoping. Move on and allow the other person to do the same.

Anyone who claims that marriage is a fifty-fifty proposition doesn't know the first thing about women or fractions.

HARD TO GET
OR PLAYING IT SMART

ഌ൭C൞

To a smart girl, men are no problem. To a smart girl, a man is the answer!

Does the *shidduch* system eliminate the challenge - an important element of dating? Wanting someone who seems hard to get may make you attracted to him. But is this challenge virtually eliminated within the framework of the *shidduch* system?

After both sides agree to go out, with everyone reporting back to the *shadchan* as soon as possible, the challenge is gone sometimes. There is no feeling of mystery, and the drawn out time period of wondering and hoping that the other person is interested is eliminated. However, everyone knows they are out for *tachlis*.

In some circles, where one is allowed only a short time to get to know one another, there is no time to play games. Both parties know why they are there, and it's not to find out the weather. Each one has a limited time to ask the questions they want to ask and find out the answers they want to know. There is no acting "hard to get".

However, in every dating system there is a need to play it smart. This may mean playing hard to get, or understanding the situation and being smart about handling it.

Rhoda told her sister to play hard to get, be a challenge, and "play the game". Her sister said, "Rhoda, how can you say that? When you were going out with your husband you did not play hard to get, you were not a challenge and you did not play games. You were open, honest and straightforward with your husband." "Yes," answered Rhoda, "You are right. I didn't play hard to get, but that was my strategy. That was the game. I realized my husband needed someone open, honest and straight forward, so that is what I was."

You don't have to play hard to get. Rather determine a strategy and play smart. Playing hard to get is only one strategy.

Most people claim they don't want a challenge or someone who plays games. Yet many people, even without realizing it, do need a challenge and do play some kind of mind game or work out some sort of strategy.

A good wife laughs at her husband's jokes, not because they are clever, but because she is.

Even in the *shidduch* world, you have to chase the person if you want to get him. The first challenge is getting a person to agree to go out with you. If s/he refuses, you have to find people to push for you. Sometimes you can do this. Sometimes you need other people to subtly suggest it as if it were their own idea.

In more open minded *shidduch* circles, if the boy is still uninterested, a girl can go to a place where he might notice her or where a mutual friend can point her out to him. The girl's relatives - or in some circles the girl herself - can strike up an innocent conversation with the boy (asking directions or the time always goes over well). Later on someone can call, suggesting that the boy consider going out with the girl talking to him.

Finally, if a girl does date a boy who is not interested in seeing her again, she can casually "bump into him", or have someone invite both of them. This affords her a second chance to make a better impression. Many of us are familiar with the old adage, "All's fair in love and war." Sometimes you have to fight for what you want. Of course, don't reach a point where you sacrifice your own pride.

Why are woman wearing perfumes that smell like flowers? Men don't like flowers. I've been wearing a great scent. It's called New Car Interior. *(Rita Rudner)*

My husband's sister suggested I date her brother Kal, but hearing that I was a New Yorker, he was not interested. So my sister in law fixed me up with three of his closest friends. They were all terrific. The first one said, "If you think I'm nice, you should meet Kal." The second one said, "If you think I have a good voice, you should hear Kal sing." The last one said, "Kal is such a popular guy." That was enough for me. I had to meet this boy who wouldn't meet me because I was a New Yorker. When he visited his sister, I bought a bag of candy and visited his sister's kids. Kal couldn't refuse to meet me when his sister invited me to join them for dinner. Once I got my foot in the door, I could get into his life.

There is always a plan and strategy, even if it is only planning what to wear. One measures how forward to be or how much to hold back, how fast to let the relationship progress or how slow to take it. This depends on your personality and needs as well as the needs and personality of the person you are dating.

Sometimes, the boy wants to ask the girl out again on the date; or the girl wants to ask the boy whether he feels it was a good date. When a couple feels very comfortable they will discuss dating again even on the first date. It can help to let the other person wonder for a while, building a healthy anxiety. Then his mind registers that s/he likes the other person and hopes s/he agrees to another date. A couple does not discuss seeing one another again on the first few dates, if you adhere strictly to the *shidduch* rules. This automatically gives each person time to hope the other one will report positively to the *shadchan*.

I am not suggesting that you frustrate the other person. Be reliable. Call when you arranged to do so. However don't show your emotions too soon, making yourself vulnerable early in the relationship. Give a girl time to hope you will call, a boy time to wonder if you are interested. If you seem too ready or too aggressive, you may scare someone.

Play it by ear however. If your date is nervous, insecure, or turned off by a challenge, sum up the situation and do what is appropriate.

Be yourself, being open and honest and straightforward, if you're comfortable with that. But also be aware of the right approach for the person you are dating, and what makes him feel comfortable or challenged.

Some people are hard to get though they don't realize it. Individuals unable to commit for a variety of reasons - not ready, not sure, wants to meet others, hasn't gotten dating out of his system, wants to do comparative shopping, came from parents with a bad marriage etc. - often present themselves as more challenging.

When a man opens the door of his car for his wife, you can be sure of one thing - either the car or the wife is new.

One challenge is a boy whom a girl has to work hard to get. Men and women who are not warm and loving seem to be more of a challenge. Challenges can make a person seem desirable. Human beings often want what they can't have, and a rejection awakens that instinct. Don't blind yourself by the excitement of the challenge. If you do win the challenge and get the boy or girl, you are stuck with that boy or girl. Make sure s/he's the person you want. Don't win the game; be the winner.

Not everyone wants someone who gives them a difficult time. Most people are happier with someone warm and loving. After you determine that you are right for him/her, learn how to make him/her want you. What does it take? Don't be phony. Be smart.

Some people don't appreciate what they have, until they lose it. With this type of person, you may need to break up and see someone else, before s/he realizes that s/he misses you and wants you back.

Everyone needs a wake up call every so often. A husband and wife must remember to value one another, not taking each other for granted.

I went out with my mother one night while I was dating my husband. When Kal called, he was told I was out. Later, I told him I had a great evening but avoided saying with whom I had been. I didn't want to hurt him, rather to help him realize how he felt about me. It did awaken his feelings!

Adina, a warm, lovely girl was seeing Barry. Because she was inexperienced and didn't know how to verbalize or show her feelings, Barry felt she didn't like him. He told the *shadchan* Adina wasn't warm or expressive enough. The *shadchan* told Adina to memorize ten nice things she felt about Barry, and somehow tell them to Barry in the course of conversation. Adina's grandfather made Adina practice putting these thoughts into conversations. He role played Barry saying, "I had a good time." Adina answered, "So did I." "No," corrected her grandfather. "You have a boy who needs to know how you feel. Say, 'I also had a good time because you are fun to be with.' If he says, 'Do you want to go out again?' Don't just say, 'Yes.' Say, 'Of course. I really enjoy being with you. You make me laugh.'" Adina was taught to play it smart, and now they are married. They are comfortable and open with each other and each has a warm loving partner.

The best way to win an argument with a wife is to hit her over the head with a mink coat.

My husband Kal liked me but wasn't ready to get married. We had dated a few times when he came to New York from Chicago. I was scheduled to go to Grossinger's Hotel for *Shavuos* but my brother-in-law (whose wife had originally set us up) told my husband to invite me to his family in Chicago instead. My future brother-in-law convinced Kal I was vulnerable and might settle for someone not right for me. Believing this, my husband invited me. I went.

Kal warned me he was not ready for a commitment. He told me, "We can have a great time together as long as you don't take the relationship seriously." Eight children and five grandchildren later, I still tell him, "Don't worry. I'm not taking it seriously." Kal wanted us just to enjoy the holiday. We did. When it was over, my future sister-in-law, wisely asked me to stay one more day to help her buy dishes. I agreed to stay. The next day, she asked me to help her choose curtains. I agreed. Skillfully, my future sister-in-law and I did this impromptu little skit for twelve days; Kal continually asked me when I was leaving and I good naturedly answered I had promised to help his sister-in-law pick out cutlery. Kal enjoyed being with me, but he felt pressured by his family who wanted him to make a commitment to me. Though I was crazy about him, I told him not to let his family pressure him into something when he wasn't ready.

Finally, I announced that I was leaving and going back to work. Kal was confused because it was Memorial Day and I had the day off. He wondered why I couldn't stay through Memorial Day if I'd already missed so much work. But I insisted on leaving. My parents asked me the same question and I explained that I left because that was the first day Kal wanted me to stay. Five minutes after I walked through my front door the phone rang. It was Kal, and I knew I had "got him". I had played it smart, realizing Kal needed to see how sad he was without me. I wasn't fooling him. Rather I was helping him tune in to his feelings. Kal says it was the smartest thing he ever did. It certainly was the smartest thing I ever did.

Ellen liked Alan, who was in law school with her, but only as a friend. Then her friend said, "You had better decide now if you are interested in Alan because he plans to date Tammy." Ellen, suddenly aware that she could lose Alan to someone else, re-evaluated and decided she couldn't give him up. She subtly let him know and now they are married.

This unbelievable story really happened. Eric was interested in Shaina but found out that she was seriously dating David. He also found out where the date would be. Eric went there also, complete with a friend of his dressed up as a girl and posing as his date, to make Shaina jealous. Shaina saw Eric in the hotel lobby on a "date" and immediately woke up, realizing she had feelings for Eric. He played it smart. Eric was the next boy Shaina dated - and the last.

A boy chases a girl until she turns around and catches him.

Be smart, play smart, but don't misrepresent yourself. If you are not warm and gentle, don't act warm and gentle to get a person, unless you intend to play the part for the rest of your life.

Don't be outsmarted. Don't be captivated by someone in response to the challenge. Delve deep and get to know a person well. Know how to play it smart to get the person you want, and be smart so you want and are wanted by the person you get.

"I haven't spoken to my wife in years. I didn't want to interrupt her." *(Rodney Dangerfield)*

YOU NEVER KNOW

When Harry returned from his honeymoon he said, "I feel like a new man." And his wife added, "So do I."

People don't know what they are looking for until they find it. Often they meet someone and feel – "You are everything I never knew I always wanted."

A boy at his wedding carried a sign saying, "You never know."

"Paper matches" - matches that work perfectly on paper - often do not work, while matches that make no sense on paper, often work out perfectly. Elements such as timing and chemistry can not be anticipated or accounted for by other people.

Though people may think they know what they want, you never know whom you will fall for. Be flexible about whom you date because you never know.

Naomi and Stuie both speak very fast. When they first met, both talked through the other one's sentences, and both figured it would never work between them. But somehow, they hear and like one another though both still talk and answer fast. They are alike, and despite the saying "opposites attract," they are attracted to each other. It is not whether your personalities are alike but whether your outlook and goals are alike that makes for a strong marriage.

Actually, most people wouldn't put any couple together. Had my husband and I thoroughly researched each other, we would not have dated. I wasn't dating anyone who wanted me to relocate, while my husband only wanted a girl who would live in Chicago, where he was studying. I never asked where he planned to live, assuming he'd move to New York. (His parents lived in Pennsylvania.) When I called my mother to tell her I was engaged, she asked where we were going to live. I said, "New York" and my husband said, "Chicago." We first lived in Chicago and then moved to New York. Had you asked people if we were for each other, the answer would probably have been, "She's an outgoing New Yorker, and he's a quiet Southern boy. Her family is in business. His father is a Rabbi. How can you put them together?" Yet no one can tear us apart.

Raizee fixed up a girl from Queens with a Ph.D., whose family had a TV in the home, with a boy from Lakewood who never went to college. Raizee fixed them up, ignoring all their differences, because the girl and the boy were both overweight. Each has a great sense of humor and wonderful values in common. Had she researched it, she would not have matched them up, but she didn't, and it worked out great.

Lauren was in a clothing store when she overheard someone say her son was modern and therefore finding *shidduchim* difficult. He was looking for someone who would wear pants and not necessarily cover her hair. The following Friday, she hosted a *Shabbos* guest for a neighbor, and the girl wore pants. Immediately Lauren set her up with this boy. They are to be married in July.

Duvi, an outgoing boy, was always set up with outgoing girls. When he was finally fixed up with a quiet girl, he loved it. Nora had been looking for a quiet reserved boy, yet she liked Duvi. "Why?" I asked. Duvi said, "Nora listens when I speak. I don't have to compete with her for the floor." Nora said she always felt uncomfortable when her friends made sharp remarks. Now she turns to her husband and says, "Answer them." These two had no idea they were looking for their complement, but they were happy when they found it.

My daughter was fixed up with her husband who was a new *baal teshuva*. Though everyone agreed he was terrific, and had great growth potential, they also agreed he was not for my *Michlala* educated daughter; they seemed worlds apart. At that time he was learning in Israel. He wrote her a letter describing himself: he had studied Chinese as well as economics, math and philosophy, and he had planned to travel to India but had become interested in Judaism. He was not the boy my daughter was looking for and we turned down the *shidduch*. Four months later, in Israel for *Succos*, we were invited to a friend's home for dinner. These friends insisted we come because a family of *baalei teshuva* would be there as well, and it was important they meet other religious families. It turned out they were my future son-in-law and his family. My daughter and he spoke and recognized great qualities in each other. Who would have put them together? G-d did!

Gail agreed to date Aryeh after discussions had already started regarding another *shidduch*. She was uncomfortable but since Aryeh had already been informed she would go out with him, she dated out of courtesy. She also became engaged to him.

Esther dated Raphy on and off for close to a year. Something made her unsure about committing. Each time they broke up, people figured it would never come to be. Raphy was patient, good natured and understanding about her concerns. Seeing this wonderful quality in him, finally made her realize how special he was and she happily married him.

You might consider looking at friend from a new perspective. When a name is suggested, don't automatically say, "I already know her." Rethink your view of this person. You never know.

Aaron was nearing thirty, and had dated a lot, but never found the girl of his dreams. His father and Sarah's father had been good friends since they were young and Aaron had been a guest at Sarah's parent's *Shabbos* table many times. He had known Sarah for years. When Aaron's *Rav* suggested Aaron go out with Sarah, they suddenly viewed each other in a new light. They are married.

My grandmother set me up with two great dates. I watched one in the making. I was down in Florida with my grandmother and after *shul* she asked a friend, "Do you have someone special for this outstanding girl?" I wanted to die, but the friend answered, "Do I have a special boy! You should see my grandson." My grandmother expounded on my virtues and the woman matched her. My grandmother enthused about my relations and so did her friend. I just wanted to escape. Finally the woman said, "Here's my grandson's number. Tell him I told you to call." I figured the boy would be a real loser, so when my grandmother took out the phone number after *Shabbos*, saying, "Are you calling him or am I?" I said, "I'm certainly not calling." She began speaking and I hesitantly took the phone. We went out with each other as a favor to our grandmothers. He turned out to be one of my best dates, though he wasn't for me. It proved that if grandmothers have something in common, their grandchildren might, too.

This doesn't mean it's smart to throw anyone together. Marsha was fixed up with a boy who owned a showy car. He was well off and said things like, "Everyone doesn't need to go to college," and "Age doesn't matter." Marsha was 19, and he was 32. He also said, "His divorce doesn't matter." Then he said, "His son is hardly home so he doesn't matter." The only thing that really mattered to Marsha was the *shadchan* who fixed her up with this boy. What had she been thinking?

When a *shidduch* is suggested to you, have total faith in the person who is setting you up or do some research. Don't reject people lightly. Give them a chance, as you would like someone to give you a chance. And remember, you never know.

Love is an unusual game. There are either two winners or there is none.

PRESSURE

Why should I feel pressured? Today, two people asked me to get married. Unfortunately, they were my mother and father.

Pressure is the catch phrase for this time period. Everyone feels stressed, because we all want the best husband or wife, the best daughter-in-law or son-in-law. Everyone worries about whom they will marry. That choice shapes the rest of your life.

Everyone has common fears, common prayers, common hopes and common dreams. Dating and making a commitment are nerve wracking. A lot of people decide too fast, scared to be left behind while many of their friends are getting engaged. A girl once jokingly said, "Boys have to stop getting engaged without me." She didn't want to marry any of those boys, but she disliked the pressure of having people around her getting engaged. It's a common feeling, but don't pressure yourself into compromise.

Hanoch Teller, the famous storyteller, is well known for saying, "The only people who are really happy are those you don't know well." Don't envy anyone because you never know what anyone else is feeling or experiencing. Don't watch other people and rush into something just because they did. Sometimes, the seemingly happiest couples divorce. Be certain this relationship is what you want.

Don't let the pressure get to you. Get to know the person you're dating and make sure s/he gets to know you. Don't rush yourself and don't rush him/her. Have a long dating period, a short engagement period and a very long marriage.

Someone asked me, "Do I have to compromise on my dreams? Everyone else is so sure and happy about his or her fiancé." Truthfully, though everyone will say they are happy, plenty of people are unsure, scared, nervous, insecure, confused and many even wonder if they are settling.

A large percentage of people walk down the aisle with trepidation. Before my friend sent out her daughter's invitations, she told her, "If you aren't certain, we just won't mail them out."

Gila seemed so happy as an engaged girl; then she asked me, "Do you really like him? I'm so nervous. I hope I'm doing the right thing. He's very successful, and very good to me." She was unsure, but it worked out well.

Just because you're somewhat scared doesn't mean you're doing the wrong thing. Some people marry feeling one hundred percent certain and still get divorced while others have some worries and their marriage thrives. Only time gives you the answers. But, by knowing one another's needs, fears, priorities, moods, dreams etc., as best you can and by both being as certain as you can, you increase your chances of having a successful marriage.

People ask "When should I settle?" A young girl asked me, "How fussy can I be?" People, especially at twenty years old, don't want to compromise their dreams, but most people do redefine them. My grandfather used to say, "Think twice before you throw someone away." Don't force yourself to settle but do give a person a chance. Continue dating someone whom you feel has potential and get engaged if you feel you can spend the rest of your life with this person. If the uncertainty doesn't feel like normal jitters, rather you feel the person is not for you or dislike something about him/her, the marriage can fail.

Broken engagements or broken marriages often occur when someone responds to pressure.

"Do you love me, dear?"
"Dearly, sweetheart."
"Would you die for me?"
"No, my darling, mine is an undying love."

How do you know if this is the right one? You are no longer interested in the others out there. You don't want to hear any more names suggested. You don't care whom your friends are dating. You don't rationalize your feelings. You look forward to this person's phone calls and enjoy and spending time with him or her. Hopefully, you feel happy. You don't feel you are settling. You stop analyzing each component and get excited about the total person. You may still think, s/h could be thinner or more outgoing, but it doesn't matter; her/his warmth and consideration more than compensate for these things

Compromise on superficial qualities that aren't the core of the person, but don't compromise on the way a person treats you. S/he must make you feel good about yourself. Don't allow verbal abuse to be a problem in your marriage. Everyone deserves someone who treats them as they'd like to be treated. Everyone has different needs for love, attention, dependency, even adoration. Make sure your potential spouse reaches or has the potential to reach that threshold.

"Dearest," sighed the young man, "couldn't you learn to love me?"
"I might," said the girl. "I learned to eat spinach."

Because of pressure, some people are negative and disillusioned, though many are able to stay optimistic. People enjoy being with happy, smiley, upbeat individuals, so be positive and focused. Look good, feel good and stay busy. Keep smiling and you will feel happy and find happiness. Anger and frustration feed on themselves, making you even more discouraged and bringing out the worst in the other person.

Most single people can't wait to look back at this dating period and laugh. Hopefully you too will look back, remembering only the good things about your dating experience.

Watch your health during this tense time. The *shidduch* period can be great or terrible for your diet. One father lost thirty pounds during his daughter's dating period; her mother gained twenty pounds.

My grandfather constantly asked me if I was making progress. I'd tell him about how well I was handling school, work and friends, and he'd say, "Yes, but are you making progress?" To him, a single person was only progressing if s/he found her *bashert*, got married, and raised a family. Other types of progress do exist and are worthwhile. Sometimes, girls who marry later find that having their degrees means they don't have as hard a time juggling school and a baby.

It is not a disgrace if you have not yet found your *bashert*. Though there may be a problem with someone's attitude, usually s/he has not yet been lucky enough to meet the right person. It takes some people longer. Each person has to put in his *hishtadlus* but in the end it's up to *Hashem*. Some of the best people get married later in life. It's not just important to find a person; it's important to find the right person.

We are not privy to *Hashem's* plan. One woman was still single when she turned forty. Unfortunately her sister, married with two children, developed cancer and passed away. The single woman, a nurse, was able to fully devote herself to caring for her sister during her illness. She later married her brother-in-law and became a wonderful mother to her sister's children. G-d obviously had a plan. So don't get discouraged, and learn from your own as well as other people's experiences.

There is pressure when friends and classmates get engaged, marry or have children. It feels like the world is moving on and leaving you behind. Though people are happy for their friends, they are sad for themselves, becoming disillusioned. Everyone hopes they'll do research, go out, find the right person and get married. In some lucky cases it happens that way, but sometimes it takes time. Keep the faith that your turn will come.

At Stern College an engaged girl gets a *Mazel Tov* sign on her door. It's every girl's dream to hang that sign. Holiday weekends, when there are lots of engagements and weddings, and new signs are placed all over, can be hard and depressing for those who have not yet found their mate. Their anxiety level increases.

I once dated a boy who lectured me all night about not being particular, saying I had to be realistic and settle. (I was already the ripe old age of twenty). With these tactics, the boy, whom I knew wasn't for me, convinced me to date him three times. We all become vulnerable.

He said: "I know I am not tall and handsome like Charles. I realize I am not bright and influential like Charles but, please say you will be mine. I love you and can not live without you."

She said: "I love you too but where can I find this man Charles?"

Sometimes people pose ultimatums, saying things like, "If you don't agree to marry me, it's over." Some people just needed the push, but others agree and then call off the engagement. Their "yes" was a reaction to fear rather than to their heart, which wasn't fully committed.

One of my friends resists the pressure. She wants to *daven* and wait. A *shadchan* called to fix up her daughter, and she said, "Not yet." The *shadchan* called again and she said, "Not yet." After the third call, my friend agreed to let her daughter go out with the boy just to stop the *shadchan's* calls. They got married. This works for some lucky people. Though no persistent *shadchan* made it *easy* for her when her second daughter was of age, and she had to search for her daughter's *bashert,* she maintains a wonderfully positive attitude that *everything* will work out well.

My sister Rivki, who helped edit this book, said she is grateful her kids are still young. She is exhausted just from reading how difficult the *shidduch* system is.

A real fairytale ending is: "And they lived happily <u>even</u> after!"

WAIT, DON'T GET MARRIED YET IF...

You can tell when a husband isn't handy when he asks the man next door how to get blood off a saw.

The following are not rules; they are suggestions or thoughts to consider. Think about these things, adding them into your calculations when you consider marrying someone. Don't marry someone who falls into any of these "wrong for you" categories, unless you understand the problem, have accepted the person for who s/he is, and are willing to live with and cope with the consequences.

Don't marry someone until you truly feel you want to spend a lifetime with this individual.

Don't be pushed or pressured by yourself, the other person, your parents or friends, or fear. The fear of losing someone is a catalyst pushing a person into making a commitment. Sometimes, the fear of losing someone makes you realize how much the person means to you. But, don't marry because you are afraid you won't find someone else, or because s/he may reject you, or because people tell you how silly you were to pass him or her up. Want the person; don't respond to pressure.

Don't get married if your parents are unsure. Parents are smarter than you think. They've experienced life. At least hear their concerns.

Don't get married if you are uncomfortable with something in the person's personality. If you constantly question something, and need to speak to marriage counselors or Rabbis before the wedding, something isn't right. Deal with whatever is worrying you before you get married.

Don't marry someone who doesn't meet your needs just because people promise that he wants to change or can be different. Wait until the person changes. Don't ignore the things that bother you. They show up later on in your marriage.

Don't get married because all your friends are getting married and you are afraid or embarrassed to be left by the wayside.

Don't get married if you don't know the person and his or her family well. (Would it be terrible to discover some of the skeletons in his closet before you marry?)

Don't get married if the person isn't considerate of you, or isn't sympathetic to others. A person is usually most attentive during the dating period, wanting to put his or her "best foot forward". If a boy or girl doesn't show kindness before the wedding, s/he will treat you worse after marriage. You can adjust and compromise about certain things but don't compromise about respect.

Be careful before marrying someone who doesn't have a Rebbe, mentor or someone whose guidance he respects. He will probably not listen to his wife either and she will not have anyone to turn to if disagreements arise. Meet the Rebbe to be sure he is on your wave length and that you respect the advice he gives your intended.

Try not to get married when you have just rebounded from another relationship. Wait until your emotions have calmed down. Often people grab the next person after a rejection. If a boy rejects a girl, saying she wasn't bright enough for him, the girl may marry a medical student to prove she's bright enough for a doctor, without considering whether he is kind, loving or devoted enough for her.

Don't get married for money, looks, prestigious jobs or impressive names. These things fade. Marry a person for their goodness, their *midos*, their personality, their ability to adapt, their desire to make you happy, and their love.

Don't marry someone because everyone else thinks s/he is perfect for you, or because everyone else wants him, or because you are scared there won't be anyone else.

Don't marry someone who makes you feel insecure.

Don't marry in response to a challenge. Yaron is a terrific boy and the girls flocked around him. Then he met Laura who was cold and indifferent to him. Yaron took this as a challenge and was thrilled when Laura finally broke down and agreed to marry him. Unfortunately, when the excitement of conquering a challenge was over, Yaron discovered he'd married a hard, cold girl. Laura wasn't playing hard to get – she was just being herself. Now Yaron has to deal with a tough wife.

Don't marry someone solely because he or she offers something you lack. Elsa's family was very careful about spending money. She met Joel whose family spent money lavishly. This appealed to Elsa, but though Joel's family offered generosity, they didn't offer the warmth of her family.

People from unobservant families might marry their spouse because his family is more religious. But don't just look for what you lack. This family may be more observant, but may lack sensitivity. Look at the total picture.

Yetta's father was stingy, watching every penny. Yetta married a medical student, figuring he'd have lots of money. She ignored his personality, which was to be just as frugal with his money as her father.

Don't marry someone if you are not proud of him, or don't want to be seen with him. In different circumstances, with different people – family, friends, co-workers, charity collectors – and under all types of pressures, you should feel, "I really like this person." You don't have to feel s/he is always perfect, but you have to feel s/he or she is all right, and can grow and mature.

Don't get married if you continually criticize or are being criticized by your intended. You have to like and accept him or her, and you have to feel good about yourself. Your spouse is your mirror through life. Make sure you like what you see.

Don't marry someone who uses religion to back up something he wants, that you do not want. A control freak can find a *Chazal* to back up almost anything.

Don't get married if the other person can't handle your type of life. If you enjoy your large family and hectic home, make sure s/he can handle your hectic lifestyle, and you can handle his. Does he need his freedom? Does she need alone time? Do you need someone always there for you? Know your needs. Make sure s/he meets them. Know his or her needs. Make sure you can and want to meet them.

How can you tell when a boy really doesn't have much to offer?

His bride shows up at the wedding with a date.

Don't marry the person if you can't tolerate his or her circle of friends. You will not necessarily replace them. Be sure you can be a part of them. If he can't get along with your circle of friends, figure out why. Is he just uncomfortable, or does he feel threatened by them, or competitive with them?

Don't marry a person if you haven't seen him or her in different situations, including frustrating ones. See how he reacts when you are late. See how she acts when she's tired, overtired, and under pressure. Find out what kind of temperament the person has. Your spouse may have a short temper, be stubborn or demanding, get depressed, need sleep, or become irritable when s/he is hungry. Be aware of this and accept it, if you feel his other qualities make these worth it.

Don't get married if you have major religious differences.

Don't get married if you have different uncompromising outlooks on life, child rearing, where or how you want to live, and the kind of home you'd like to have (open, hospitable, or very private). One woman, now divorced, had a husband who never allowed her friends to visit. If someone dreams of living in Israel, and s/he marries a person who refuses to consider it, this can be a major source of frustration and conflict. These dreams should be discussed before the marriage. Don't get married if your hopes and dreams aren't on the same track. They don't have to be identical, but they have to be flexible and compromising.

Don't get married if you can't speak openly and comfortably with the person. Marriage carries many challenges. You have to communicate with him.

Don't get married if you are turned off by the person's looks. You have to eat, sleep and live with this person for a long time.

Don't marry someone if you hear bad things about him. Don't necessarily believe everything you hear, but don't ignore it. Check it out. Sandra divorced her husband Jacob. Bella, Jacob's lawyer who represented him in the divorce, heard all the horrible things his ex-wife said about him. Nevertheless, Bella married him. Two children later, she realized she should not have ignored those terrible things. She too got rid of him.

Don't marry into a family if the parents are not nice to each other. Even divorced parents can treat each other civilly. If the father treats the mother nicely, you can assume the boy has learned how to treat a wife. Occasionally, a boy may have seen his mother mistreated and decided to be different from his father. There are always exceptions. Judge each person for him or herself.

Don't reject someone because s/he isn't every thing you want. It's the total person who has to appeal to you. Though every idea and ideal need not match, you must be able to work together, complement each other, sometimes balance each other, compromise with each other and grow together. (See chapter The Person) No individual will be everything you want, but remember you are gaining a person in your life, not losing the others you already have. If you enjoy singing but he can't sing, marry him anyway and sing with your friends.

People study for SATs, GREs, LSATs, or MCATs for a year or two, because it can determine their career. Study the person you are dating, her life style, his family, her hopes, his dreams. Study your feelings about that person, analyzing the timing, circumstances, and your needs. This is truly your future.

Make sure the person you are marrying meets your personal criteria. If you are counting on changing the other person, you are making a mistake!

Don't marry just because you want to be married. Chana married Shalom because he wanted to marry her, and she wanted to be married. Their marriage failed because he felt that marriage had more to offer. Chana couldn't offer it to him because she didn't love him. A person needs to feel loved and a person has to be in love to give love. It's not a one shot deal, it's a lifetime commitment!

His wife made him join a bridge club. He jumps off Tuesday.

Parents

ں)) ں

"The decision to have a child is the decision to have a piece of your heart walking around outside your body."

Have you seen a woman looking drawn and tired with bags under her eyes? Have you seen a man racing home from work nervous and finicky? Chances are this couple has a child in the *parshah*!

Parents are often overwhelmed by the entire *shidduch* period.

Parents begin the *shidduch* process as soon as their child is born. You bring your child up with good values and good *midos*, giving him a proper education, and helping him develop into a total person. It is the parent's responsibility to help a child develop their brains, looks, and personality to the fullest capacity.

Life doesn't come with an instruction book – that's why we have parents.

My daughter and I are both going out. She's going out with men and I'm going out of my mind.

A Rabbi told me he was certifiably insane while his daughter was dating, then he reminded himself that everything is in *Hashem's* hands and he calmed down.

A couple recently married off a twenty three year old daughter and a twenty year old son. They have so much free time now, they don't know what to do with their life anymore.

As a parent, your challenge is to direct your child without imposing your needs. Guide him and try to see eye to eye with him, finding a balance between what you and he want.

One woman complained to a *Rebbetzin* that her daughter abuses her for not making enough calls, or doing enough research. The *Rebbetzin* answered, "Abuse is part of a mother's job description." So is worrying.

As parents, we are continually sacrificing and struggling to make our children happy, but that's what makes us parents.

Parents must decide how open to be with their children.

Parents must know how their child will respond to their opinions. Some kids listen to everything their parents say, while some kids rebel against everything their parents say. Some kids are very influenced by their parents' opinions, some kids are only mildly influenced. Some are indifferent, while others react negatively. The dating period can be rough for the parents and the child. At this time in particular, parents must be sensitive, watch what they say, and not be overly critical.

Give your child confidence. Don't pressure your child into marriage. Have a happy heart, telling your child that there are plenty of good people and in time s/he will be blessed to meet the right one.

You may be frustrated if an inappropriate neighbor moves next door, but if you had helped them move in, you would never forgive yourself. So too, a wrong *shidduch* for your child hurts immensely, but if you misled your child you never stop blaming yourself. In this age of instant gratification parents are pressured to give their child everything, yet they must be cautious not to hurt them.

Some kids do not want their parents involved. They may feel their parents want something different than they want. They may feel they can handle it, with help from their friends or their *Yeshiva*. This issue should be discussed rationally by the child and his parents.

Other children accuse their parents of not being sufficiently involved or of not doing enough research.

Some parents are interested in everything their children do; who their teachers are, who their classmates are, who their counselors are, where they go to school, etc. Then they don't interfere about *shidduchim*.

Some parents are glad their child is dealing with these matters himself. Other parents feel frustrated or hurt at not being included. Children should be sensitive to their parents' wishes.

Who knows better, the parent or the child? Should we let children learn from their own mistakes? Dorit is unhappily married. She cried to her mother, "Why did you let me marry Richard?" Her mother answered, "What are you talking about? I begged you not to marry him. You cried and screamed that you loved him, and wanted only him." Dorit answered, "Yes Mommy. That is true. But I was only eighteen. What did I know?"

Hatzalah ran a poignant sign which read, "Behind every teenager who dies in a car accident, there is a parent who didn't say 'no.'" Parents are responsible, and should speak up if they feel something is wrong. They bear the guilt, and ache for their children who suffer.

Sometimes though, children resent their parents who refuse to respect their wishes. Parents who refuse a *shidduch* their child has chosen must be sure their reasoning is sound.

My friend is embarrassed to ask people to fix up her daughter. I continually remind her that it is her responsibility. Her daughter will be frustrated if she is not doing her job. In her conversations she can bring up the question, "Whom do you know that might be right for my daughter?"

In some circles, it was common for a nineteen year old girl to do her own dating research. She was young, energetic and excited to go out. She could stay up late into the night collecting information. Now mothers, worn out and tired with a household to run, torture themselves doing this research as part of the *shidduch* system.

Parents tell children to go out; "What do you have to lose? What are a few hours out of your life?" They often spend more hours investigating than the child spends on the date. Kids may feel the date will takes too much out of them. What about the research taking the *kishkas* (insides) out of parents?

Once, many people tried to persuade a boy to go out with someone, yet he adamantly refused. Finally, the girl's father called the boy's parents, asking if they could convince their son to date his daughter at least once. Though the boy's father did his best his son would not agree to the date.

Two friends set up their children. When the girl refused to go out a second time, her parents couldn't face their friends, the boy's parents, for quite a while. My daughter was once set up with my friend's son. After the first date, she realized he was not right for her. Nevertheless, out of courtesy, she went on a second date and ended it on a nice note.

If a boy or girl is popular, mothers are busy researching suggested names. If a boy or girl is not popular, mothers are busy calling people for suggestions, and finding people to *rhed* the *shidduch*.

A mother may hope that her daughter will get a better husband than she did, but she knows her son will never get as good a wife as his father did.

Shidduch dating is not a foolproof system and parents may still try to break it up after you have begun dating. If a girl wants a boy to stay in learning, but the parents don't, they shouldn't allow her to date someone in learning, assuming she'll change her mind. She may not, and then the parents will not be supportive. Any objections parents have should be voiced before their daughter dates the boy, and certainly before she really likes him. Of course, the child may respectfully present his views, explaining to his parents why the suggestion appeals to him. He may convince his parents to agree, allowing him to date the person he chooses.

Each date is a potential spouse. Parents and children must realize this, and not agree to someone under pressure. Avoid going out with someone whose parents have not consented to the match. It leads to problems.

People assume that everyone is happy by the time a girl and boy go out since the parents have done a lot of research. This may not be true. Firstly, parents can still be unsure. Secondly, sometimes people agree to the *shidduch* only as a reaction to the last date or because no one else is presently available. They may also have had a pre-conceived notion of the person which did not hold true once they met. Sometimes parents compromise because their child liked something s/he heard. And sometimes, you hear things that bother you after you agreed to the date. Research is good, but meeting the person is what counts. You have to judge for yourself.

It takes at least two people to make a marriage – a single girl and an anxious mother.

Parents must stay on top of the situation before they allow their kids to get engaged.

Be supportive, encouraging and excited if things are going well. But ask the questions that concern you, even if it upsets your child or puts a damper on things. Your child may hate it if you say, "But, is he mature?" or "Is he responsible?" or "Don't you think he gets a bit too nervous?" She'll jump to his defense. "Ma, he's very responsible, you make him nervous that's why he left his wallet at home." But you will make her think about whether or not he is responsible.

People hate to rock the boat, so if the courtship is going well, they hesitate to say anything. This doesn't work. The world rocks the boat sooner or later, so make sure your child is sailing through life with the right person. Question now before any commitments are made.

This is difficult because everyone wants to see the *shidduch* work. The child wants to be married; the parents want to see their child married; the grandparents are dreaming of seeing their grandchild married; and the great-grandparents are also anxiously waiting to see this child walk down the aisle. The next sibling in line wants to start dating, and is waiting for her sister. Of course the little siblings who can't tolerate their edgy parents' behavior and the commands to clean up and be well behaved when the date arrives, are rooting for it to work out also.

The boy, the girl, her parents, and her siblings all feel the tension when the boy walks through the door.

Each boy who walks through the door is "new hope" but he also brings new fears. Will he like her? Will she like him? Did we check him out enough? Did we really get the inside story on his family? Does anyone really know the truth?

My parents want me to get married. They don't care to whom any more, as long as he doesn't have a pierced ear. That's all they think about. I think men who have pierced ears are better prepared for marriage. They've experienced pain and bought jewelry. *(Rita Rudner)*

How forceful can parents be if they don't like the *shidduch*? Some parents prevent it by disapproving and telling their child they can not marry the person. In some extreme cases parents cut their children off, not supporting their child anymore, or refuse to make a wedding, or stop credit cards. These parents may be doing the right thing for their child and should be admired for their courage. Or they may cause their child pain by having different values than him and therefore not appreciate the relationship their child is experiencing. In that case they must examine their own motives. It is a parent's prerogative to do what they believe is right, however it may be advisable for them to speak to a reliable third party such as a *Rav*, a therapist or even a close relative or friend to understand each other's perspective and resolve the issue amicably.

Parents must be careful. A couple married despite the girl's parents' disapproval, however with so much negative pressure they succumbed and divorced. Immediately following the breakup they missed each other and wanted to remarry. However the boy was a *kohen* and by law, could not re-marry his wife, who was now a divorced woman.

A set of parents kept their son from marrying the girl he liked, because they were not ready for him to be married. When the girl moved on and married someone else, the boy was devastated and remained single for a long time. His parents were left with an unhappy son and spent much energy wondering whether they had truly done what was best for their son.

Parents objected to a certain boy and pressured the girl until the engagement was renounced. They wanted their daughter to marry a motivated boy, who was planning to obtain a good education and had goals they could appreciate. These parents believed this boy had too much growing to do. They loved their daughter and found it difficult to hurt her this way. The boy, who also loved this girl, rose to the occasion and proved to the girl's parents that he was worthy of their daughter. The parents were upstanding enough to recognize that he had made the effort and changes they wanted, and allowed their daughter to marry him.

Parents must examine and re-examine their own instincts. Everyone has ulterior motives. Parents see their friend's kids getting married. Mothers are tired from running a house, and fixing up a child is an added pressure. Fathers can't take coming home to nervous wives, nor do they want to rush home early to meet another potential suitor. Fathers are concerned that their sons marry into a prestigious family, for their own pride. Every parent must be certain his motives lead him in a direction best for his child.

Should a parent continue to ask the child, "are you sure", once s/he is engaged? Should you just encourage the child at that point? Do you allow the child to get caught up in the excitement of the upcoming wedding? The bottom line is, don't allow your child to marry unless you or at least your child is certain it is right. (See chapter "Don't Get Married If…")

Young, attractive Susan came home excitedly to tell her mother that she'd just become engaged. "Who is the young man?" her mother asked.

"He's a musician. Of course, he's not working right now."

"An unemployed musician? Look, don't tell your grandparents. They wouldn't understand about an unemployed musician. Neither would your father. He hates musicians. Tell him your fiancé sells soap. And don't worry about me. I'm going to the kitchen to put my head in the stove!"

YOUTH

Youth is wasted on the young.

Parents have "been there, done that", but kids don't want to learn from their parents' mistakes.

Kids often think they know it all. Unfortunately, they often outsmart themselves.

Each time you advance a stage in life, the period before seems simpler in comparison. When you are caring for a baby, the dating stage seems simple. When you are looking for a *shidduch* for your son or daughter, the teenage years seems like a cinch.

Be compassionate to those dealing with an earlier stage that you've already passed. One day you'll be at the next stage and will also reflect back, feeling this stage was simpler. Don't resent people who don't understand the stage you are presently in, and learn from the experience of those who have already gone through a more advanced stage.

"Little children, little problems - big children, big problems"

An eighteen year old girl is in the "big children" category so get lots of R&R (rest and relaxation) when your daughter is seventeen years old, because when she hits eighteen it's "get to work".

"When a child is small you carry them in your hand. When a child is big you carry them in your head."

Raising children is not all it's cracked up to be. Only you crack up.

Insanity is hereditary. You get it from your kids.

A kid goes off to college at eighteen and returns at twenty-one. He's surprised to find out how smart his parents got in three years.

Kids should listen to their parents' objections or concerns about a person they are dating. Most people still need their parent's advice after marriage. Besides it is unpleasant if your parents are critical of your spouse.

Can you call your child on his cell if he is out late on a date? As a Jewish mother, I say "yes". Exercise restraint because calling during a date may spoil a mood or make the child feel you don't trust him, or are being nosey or intrusive. But call if it's late and you're calling out of concern. It's okay if a girl knows the boy has parents who are worried, and are an important part of their child's life. Be conscious of the time if you don't want these interruptive phone calls, and make a quick call home to say things are okay and you'll be out late.

"I think I'd be a good mother. Maybe a little over protective. Like I would never let the kid out - of my body." *(Wendy Liebman)*

I asked a friend how she was doing with her daughter's *shidduch* dating.

She said, "I'll kill anyone who mentions the word *shidduch* after I marry my kids off."

I asked a grandmother what her grandson wanted.

"A girl," she answered.

"Okay," I said. "Let's start again. What does his mother want?"

I asked some one, "How are you doing with your daughter?"

She answered, "At least we haven't made any mistakes yet."

I asked some other friends how their daughter was doing.

They answered, "The good news is we're always doing." You can't win if you're not in the game.

Every mother and father has put their "all" into their child. The person their child marries often determines how close a bond remains.

It's essential to see that parents are kind to each other. Kids learn to do what they see and children often turn into their parents.

A girl's parents should meet the boy on the first date. Sometimes this doesn't work out for logistical reasons and they meet the boy at a later date. (The chapter "The Rules" discusses parents meeting the girl, the boy or their parents, either on the first date or soon after.)

According to Jewish law, children are not bound by their parents' *shidduch* preferences, yet should not do anything that embarrasses their parents. A *poseik* must be consulted if necessary.

A good relationship between parent and child is important. They should respect one another's feelings and opinions.

Attention Teenagers: If you are tired of being hassled by unreasonable parents, now is the time for action. Leave home, and pay your own way, while you still know everything!

TIMING

"Life is what happens while you are busy making other plans."

Timing is a major ingredient in whom you marry.

A boy once said to me, "If you aren't going to marry me, you will make some other girl very happy." He got engaged the following week. He was ready for marriage.

One short period in time and one decision of whom to marry determines the rest of your life. It's part *mazel*, timing, your state of mind, outside pressures, inner pressures and of course emotions and intellect. Your desire to marry may override your intellect or vice versa. Attraction may override your intellect or it may sustain the marriage. (My humorous friend with a good-looking husband always says, "He's not much in the brains department, but isn't he gorgeous?" Their marriage seems to work.) Someone may overwhelm you, impress you, intimidate you, or be right for you. Sometimes you can be so impressed that the other person is interested in you, that you don't realize s/he is not right for you. Maybe your friends are getting married and you don't want to be left behind, or you've finished school and don't know what to do, so this person is a solution. Whatever the reasons to marry, certainly this one decision determines the rest of your life.

It's important to be in the right place at the right time. Being the first name on a person's list can give you the advantage. Many people do marry their first date. The person is excited to be dating and happy to find someone they like. They don't have a basis of comparison, and are not looking for a combination of every appealing thing they ever saw in their previous dates.

Parents may get nervous when their child likes the first person s/he dated. One woman told her son, "A girl is not like a shirt. You don't buy the first one you try on." But truthfully, many of these marriages work out well and the people involved can be grateful they didn't suffer a long dating process.

Sometimes, being his/her first date works against you. The boy or girl may feel s/he has no basis of comparison. S/he may not appreciate the special qualities of the date, assuming every one possesses those qualities. After a person dates for a while, s/he learns to appreciate those qualities in a person.

I was attracted to self-centered guitar playing boys who loved attention, but I didn't want to marry a self-centered person, so I decided to speak to someone. The very next day I met my husband who plays the guitar, yet is sweet, kind, fine, and as far from self-centered as they come. I was crazy about him immediately and never had to start any sessions. Life is all timing.

Loni dated a boy but his family was against the *shidduch*. The parents of the next boy she met loved her. That helped her decide to marry him. When you stop dating a tough boy, you want to date a nicer person. When you stop seeing a girl who hurt your confidence, you want to date someone who boosts your ego. It's timing and it can work for you or against you. If it makes you find what is right for you, it's great timing.

Girls often start dating even though an older sister may be unmarried. Yet, even if they meet the right boy, they may feel too much guilt to get engaged. Here timing works against them.

People often get engaged soon after losing close relatives. Maybe it's coincidental, perhaps the deceased relative is working for them at a higher level, and possibly the timing is right; they need someone to fill the void.

What do you call a widower? A *chassan*. A grieving lonely widower is ripe for re-marriage. I wanted to fix up a widower when he was "ready to date". He was married before I ever imagined he would be ready to date.

There was a case where one woman paid a *Shivah* (condolence) call to a man who had lost his wife. She visited him every day of the *Shivah*. On the last day, when he got up to return to work, she was outside waiting to drive him there. He married her. Her timing was perfect.

Marsha said she didn't care about money. On a rainy night she dated a boy who dragged her on and off buses. Her next date arrived in a beautiful car. She married him despite being incompatible in many areas.

Date long enough to know it's not only timing or a reaction to events or other people that make you want to marry this one. Marry this person because s/he is what you want. The timing has to be right, but so does the person.

It's him, it's the two of you together, its timing, it's G-d.

After a quarrel a wife said to her husband, "You know, I was a fool when I married you."

The husband replied, "Yes dear, but I was in love and didn't notice it."

ISRAEL

Israel had just become independent and was short
of all military supplies. One American tried to enlist,
but was turned down. They had no uniform for him.
Trying the air force, he was again turned down. The
air force had no planes. The American tried to join
the Israeli navy. The recruiting sergeant asked, "Do
you swim?" The American said, "Don't you have any
ships either?"

The decision to move to Israel is beautiful and noble, although
not always realistic. Young adults who return from studying in Israel
are enamored with the *Kedushah* they experienced there. They love

228 • THE ART OF THE DATE

the wonderful feeling of being in the Holy Land. They feel they are in the right place, doing the right thing.

They enjoy the *shiurim* offered by outstanding Rabbis, *Rebbetzins* and scholars. Practically everyone they meet is Jewish, and they always feel like they are socializing. In New York, you're excited if the cab driver is Israeli. In Israel you can always choose to drive with Israeli cab drivers. The boy at the bagel store, the bus driver and the ambulance driver are all your Jewish brethren.

Furthermore, the independence which many teenagers experience for the first time is an awesome feeling. They are on their own, growing in maturity and spirituality. Most non-Israeli kids are students of the same age with a common bond, contributing to the appeal of Israel.

These young adults are offered a wonderful opportunity. They enjoy the benefits of being in Israel without the concerns of long-term settlement. They may miss their families but know they are in Israel for a limited time. They busy themselves enjoying the temporary escape and immerse themselves in learning, touring, visiting and strengthening their souls and their senses.

Most of these young adults do not concern themselves with financial issues, which is a major problem for long-term settlers.

During this year or two in Israel, many kids are enthralled with Israel and decide they wish to live there. When they return to the U.S.A. and begin dating, they often refuse to date anyone who will not commit to moving to Israel.

Although at this point they are committed to *aliyah*, circumstances can make this move difficult. Girls are overwhelmed by having babies far away from their mothers. Boys often find it hard to make a living. (Boys who do not work, but rather continue learning, often survive in Israel for a longer period of time.) Parents, who miss their kids and feel bad missing out on the *nachas* of enjoying their grandchildren, pressure their children to move back to the U.S.

Some young couples settle successfully in Israel, but the majority enjoys a few years there and then return home. The successful couples often have one set of in-laws who live in Israel, or they are unbelievably determined. Girls or boys, who are not one hundred percent certain about a long-term move, must make their reservations known to the person they are dating. If the person is not flexible about this issue, perhaps s/he should date someone else.

Girls or boys who want to live in Israel should date other people who share this interest. Both must understand that if one is unhappy the other would respect the wish to move back. Being flexible and compromising is a key to a good marriage.

Shana made *aliyah* on her own. My eldest son wanted to try living in Israel, but I did not encourage him to date Shana since she had already committed to *aliyah*. After he married, Shana moved back to the States. Someone suggested her for my next son, but I had the opposite problem now. This son also wanted to try living in Israel and Shana no longer wanted that.

Israel can't be the only factor when you decide whom you will marry. Many young people say they are moving to Israel, but actually don't. One boy only dated girls who committed to *aliyah*. One girl was willing to try it, but could not guarantee she would never want to return. They broke up. He married another girl who had no real desire to make *aliyah*, but said she would if he insisted. Due to circumstances, they never moved. A couple of years later, they divorced. Ironically, he didn't make *aliyah*. She did!

It is not uncommon for someone to stay in the States, though he planned to move to Israel, while someone else who never thought to move to Israel, winds up living there. Miriam refused to date anyone who voiced even a slight interest in living in Israel. Her seminary year had not been that positive and she felt she had already spent enough time in Israel. When she married Dave they both wanted to live in New York, the center of action, only spending the first few months of their marriage in Israel, to be on their own for a bit. They are now starting their fourth year there.

Aliyah is a beautiful dream and for many it will hopefully become a reality. We all pray that *Moshiach* come soon, quickly in our time, so that we can move to *Eretz Yisroel* together. But, for the time being, young couples should realize the difficulties, keeping that in mind when dating and demanding that the other person be ready to make the transition.

Couples may love Israel, but soon realize that life was simpler as a young *Yeshiva* student away from home, than as newlyweds setting up a home and building a new life. And since many of the neighborhoods are transitional, with new couples moving in but others returning home, it can be lonely for those left behind.

One girl told me spending a year or two in Israel as a young married couple is important because you grow together, learning to depend on one another. I agree but it is lonely for the parents here and for the newlyweds. This girl had gotten married at the end of the summer and moved to Israel after the *Yamim Tovim*. She and her husband didn't go back after Pesach, so her year in Israel started in November and ended in March. I told her, "A four month year is about what I can handle for my children." My daughter and son-in-law remained in Israel for two and a half years but we did, thankfully, fly back and forth to spend time together.

I love Israel and admire anyone who moves there. I would move there too if my entire family went with me. I admire anyone who can leave their family but I also feel sorry for them (unless of course they travel back and forth extensively). They are gaining a lot but also missing out on so much. Family love and closeness is irreplaceable. Of course, with cell phones and easy travel people do manage to stay close.

One's feelings about Israel must be considered, but be realistic about the feasibility of the dream and whether the person you are dating shares that dream. Don't base your decision to date someone on their feelings about *Aliyah*. Meet someone who sounds right for you, even if s/he can't be one hundred percent certain about *Aliyah*. Two people who are right for one another, can shape and achieve a common dream together.

If you want my final opinion of the mystery of life and all that, I can give it to you in a nutshell. The universe is like a safe to which there is a combination. But the combination is locked up in the safe. *(Peter Devries)*

SUPPORT

A father interviews a potential son-in-law.

"How will you live?" The boy says, "G-d will help."

"How will you support my daughter?" The boy answers, "G-d will help."

"How will you support your kids?" The boy answers, "G-d will help."

The daughter then asks her father, "What do you think of this boy?" The father says, "I think he's great. He thinks I'm G-d."

When a young couple is either still in school, or the husband is involved in Torah learning and does not plan to work the question of support arises. Who will support this couple? Many kids do not realize what it means to raise and support a family. They think they will automatically have what their parents have, not realizing the work and effort their parents put into establishing their home and life. They also don't realize how much everything costs. Everyday living expenses include rent for an apartment, phone bills, electric and gas bills, home improvements, decorating, furnishing and bedding, utensils, and food. What about having company? (The cost of preparing a *Shabbos* meal can be mind-blowing for a young couple). Items like tissues, toilet paper and paper towels add up. Transportation, whether by car, train, or car services, plus entertainment, renting movies, and eating out all add up to a big bill. Necessities like eyeglasses, lenses, *Seforim*, clothing, coats, shoes, cameras, film, and simple school supplies that your parents always had and you never thought about also cost money. A house, a car, and vacations which many people consider necessities become luxuries when you can't afford them. People can live on more or less but not on nothing. This subject must be thoroughly explored with the in-laws and the couple.

In circumstances where the couple can not support themselves at the present time or in the foreseeable future, support should be discussed before the relationship becomes serious.

Support should be defined. Often people tell the *shadchan* they can help the kids. What does that mean? People have different ideas of support. It can mean giving the couple a small minimal allowance per week for the first year, or it can mean buying them a car, a house, and paying for their grandchildren's education. It does matter! It is the source of a lot of friction, worry and problems.

Who is going to support them? The girl's parents? The boy's parents? Both sets of parents equally? Each set according to their means? Will the boy work and help support? Can the boy work and still learn as much as he'd like? Is he going into *chinuch*? Does the *kollel* pay a sufficient amount to live? Will the girl work and to what extent? Will she be able to make her own hours so she can raise a family?

How will parents' support be given? Will there be an allowance? Unfortunately, most people are too embarrassed to discuss finances so it becomes a problem later on. Don't assume anything. I've heard of wealthy people who are reluctant to help their kids financially while people of minimal means do whatever they must to help their children and vice versa.

Sometimes the *shadchan* works this out before the first date is arranged. The *shadchan* may call and say the girl is wonderful but her parents can't even afford to make a wedding. Know your own circumstances and situation. If you can afford it, the girl may be worth it.

"Most people spend eight hours earning money, eight hours spending money, eight hours spending more than they earn and eight hours wondering why they can't sleep." *(Toni Salerno)*

Some people take on extra jobs to help out their kids. A mother of eleven children took a part time job to help support her eldest daughter and son-in-law who is learning in *yeshiva*. That may be fine for one child but what will this woman do when her other children need help?

Some marriages are like mergers where each side makes sure their children are well supported.

Some people are more anxious about money for support or a family business for the boy to go into, than the qualities of the person they are dating.

Living well is a priority for some people, and they only look for money. It is well known that, "if you marry for money, you pay for it."

Wendy married a wealthy man. Before the marriage he gave her everything, including a car. He promised her the world. After the marriage, he made her account for every cent she spent – she spent her money filing for a divorce. Make sure you know the person. Don't fool yourself or you'll find that you're the fool.

There are circles, or individuals from certain circles, who would rather live with very little than give up learning full time. A popular joke says, "Did you hear the terrible news? A girl in Boro Park got engaged to a boy who works."

Some boys have price tags on their heads. Find this out in advance. Your daughter may like a boy when suddenly the *shadchan* calls, "If this works out, the boy's parents expect you to give them a car, a house or a set amount of money."

A good learner is in demand. It often seems that no one cares about his other qualities and/or whether he will be able to support a family. Boys from modest homes can marry girls with money. Good boys are in demand because there are supposedly less good boys than good girls (though I've met lots of both.) Maybe it's because, though there are lots of available boys, they can marry the available girls or wait and marry any of these young girls or a "new crop" during the next ten years. For these reasons, many boys or their parents feel the boy is entitled to be supported by the girl's side.

One man asks another, "How's your son-in-law doing?" The other answers, "Very well. He already has five people working for him - me, my wife, his wife, his mother and his father." This boy is living by "the sweat of his father-in-law's brow".

One boy told the *shadchan* he wanted three years support while he was learning. The girl's parents agreed to this. Then the boy reconsidered and said he needed five years support. Again the girl's parents agreed. The boy then asked for ten years and again the girl's parents reluctantly agreed. The boy finally called back and said he would like life support to which the girl's parents answered, "If he wants life support let him go to the hospital. There they will be glad to put him on life support."

Adam asked me to arrange a *shidduch* for his son. Because he was paying for his daughter's wedding and son-in-law's education, he wanted the girl's parents to pay for his son's wedding and support the couple including his son's education, if this *shidduch* worked. I wondered if it could be a shared burden, but Adam said, "Mention the *shidduch* to them with my terms." Though I find it ridiculous to support one's son-in-law but refuse to help one's own son, Adam's situation is common. Of course, since Adam has more boys than girl, this policy should work in his favor.

Some boys come with debts and future bills, but they are offered as an investment. The girl's parents will have to pay for medical school or law school but one day they'll have a doctor or a lawyer for a son-in-law.

On the other hand, as soon as Ronit married Elliot, Ronit's mother sent him all Ronit's college debts. Elliot was nice and quietly paid them.

Some people are glad to give support. They want a son-in-law to learn or to go to graduate school, and they are willing to pay for it. Know what you can afford and what your values are. Just because you can support your children forever, (which is rare, unless you have very few kids and very few grandchildren), you may still value the idea that children become financially independent.

My parents did a radio show called "The Voice of Wisdom" and one night the topic was *shidduchim*. Someone complained that the boy his daughter was seeing asked for ten years of support, so he could stay in Torah learning. His daughter stopped seeing this boy. Another man called in who admired a boy willing to learn for ten years, and he wanted this boy to go out with his daughter. He added that he would be happy to support a noble boy like that. What turns off one person, can greatly appeal someone else.

The question of *Torah U'Madda* (learning and working) versus only learning, is a highly debated topic. Even boys who just learn should be prepared to teach or be equipped for some job in the event they have to support their wife and kids one day.

Some people think learning is a beautiful way to live, while others agree but think it's not realistic.

Couples who believe parents can support them and their children forever, discover they are living in a dream world. Couples who believe the wife can support the family while also caring for children and a home will find a very tired wife. Teaching is very time consuming. Making *sheitels* requires time, concentration, strength and space. In today's society, with both parents involved in their own education and careers, both should share in the raising of the children and in the house chores. Working together to contribute financial support and to run the home is essential to a good marriage. Psychological support is also important.

There are hundreds of girls in Flatbush looking for *shidduchim*. They say there are six good girls for every good boy. Some great girls marry mediocre boys. Most girls prepare to make a *parnassa*, while the boys who are in learning are not trained to make a living. They rely on their wives. It is important to encourage boys to go into *chinuch* or develop skills in computer, carpentry, business, etc. so they can contribute to the family earnings, even with a part-time job.

Sometimes it is easier when one side announces right away that they can't help with support. The other side may be frustrated but if they accept it, they are not continually aggravated. If one side believes the other side can help but won't, there is a lot of frustration.

There can be stress even when both sides agree to share the burden equally. Each side may have a different idea of how well their children should live. This must also be discussed.

In-laws who fight are a major source of conflict for a young couple. Work out what each side can and will contribute, what the couple themselves will contribute and what the couple really needs.

One woman helps support her kids according to the level they plan to eventually continue. Her son-in-law hopes to be a *Rebbe* in Israel. Ida believes her daughter will not be able to afford a car or hire help. Therefore, Ida will not buy them a car or pay for any help for them.

She feels this would be a disservice because they would become used to something they won't be able to afford themselves. Other parents believe in giving their children everything they can for as long as they can. Neither approach is inherently right or wrong. Each person has to do what he believes works for him and his children.

A system that seems to be working without too much stress developed in the Stern College/ Yeshiva University community for young college kids who want to get married. They get an apartment in Washington Heights near Y.U. The girl takes the shuttle to Stern College. They eat their meals in the Y.U. cafeteria. The cost of an apartment is not that much greater than their dorm rooms. Each one's education is still paid for by his or her parents - which most parents are willing to do. As long as the couple doesn't start a family too soon, this system works pretty smoothly.

The girl and boy must agree on whether they want a kollel life of only learning or some sort of combination of work and learning.

Yaaron had a difficult time finding a girl to marry. He wanted to support a wife but he had not yet decided on a career, so he had trouble getting dates. He said, "It is so strange. Were I to tell people I planned to learn forever, plenty of girls would date me despite the fact that I would not support. But because I will work, the girls want to be sure they are supported well."

There are girls who only want their husbands to learn. However, if they were not brought up in a learning family, they may find it difficult. If it is hard on the wife, it is hard on the husband and vice versa.

Many girls who are idealistic and want a learning boy, still want some of the niceties they grew up with, such as a nice car. These girls think they are willing to sacrifice a diamond for appliances like a washing machine and dryer. But in reality they want and certainly deserve a ring. They don't want to be asked, "Can we see your gorgeous washing machine you got for your engagement?" When this type of girl does receive a ring, she may say she didn't want it.

She may say she'll even hock it somewhere down the line. Sure, if they chop off her finger with it.

The couple and their parents should work together to figure out what is best for the newlyweds.

Freeda was seeing someone who both worked and learned. Her father wanted her to marry someone who learned full time and therefore made her break up with Evan and marry someone who learned full time. A year later, divorced and with a baby, Freeda married Evan. Her ex-husband, whom she married because he was going to devote his life to learning, went to law school. Sometimes boys, who say they will only learn, end up working while boys who plan to work full time end up learning. It depends both on their convictions and circumstances.

Couples wind up where their *parnassa* is.

I phoned a *shadchan* about a girl. He said, "I heard she doesn't have money." I answered, "Lots of people don't have money. Fix her up with someone who also doesn't have money or with someone who has money and isn't looking for it." This *shadchan* thought I was crazy and preferred not to fix her up at all.

Rena didn't want a stingy boy like her father so she married a doctor. He turned out to be a real miser. Money doesn't make someone generous. Some people have very little, and will give you the shirt off their back. Some people have lots of money, but want to accumulate it. See a person for what he is. Don't fool yourself.

Husband: "Another new dress? So ask me how I can find the money to pay for it?"
Wife: "Darling, you know I'm not inquisitive."

Remember to judge each person for his or her self. A wealthy girl can have frugal parents. A girl can be a JAP and need a lot of pampering. A wealthy girl with great values can work hard and appreciate the value of money and have generous parents. A girl of modest means can be outstanding and though she contributes very little monetarily, she requires very little. Another girl of modest means may feel deprived and want a lot. Don't reject a person for being too poor or too rich (both of which are often done). It's a package deal – find out all you can about the person and then judge if he or she is for you. Don't judge a person by their pocket. Find the best total person.

A lot of people wonder how you know if you're really in love. Just ask yourself this one question: "Would I mind being financially destroyed by this person?"

IN-LAWS

"Mixed emotions is watching your mother-in-law drive off a cliff in your new car."

What happens if you miss your mother-in-law? Reload and shoot again.

A man took his son to meet his future father-in-law. He said to his son, "Do you know who is going to be your father-in-law?" In a room of one hundred men, the boy was able to point him out immediately. The father asked, "How did you know?" The son answers, "Because I hate him already!"

One cannibal said to the other, "I hate my mother-in-law." The second one answered, "So eat the vegetables."

Two mothers-in-law meet a train on which their future sons-in-law, whom they have never seen, are arriving from Europe. Only one son-in-law descends from the train. One boy did not survive the journey. Each woman argues that he is her son-in-law. They go to King Solomon who says, "Cut him in half." The first woman starts screaming. "No, No. Don't hurt him." The second woman says, "Fine, cut him in half." King Solomon says, "Give him to the second woman. She's a real mother-in-law."

Behind every successful man, you will find an exhausted woman and a very surprised mother-in-law.

"Darling, I'd like to marry you."

"Have you seen my father?"

"Lots of times. But I still want to marry you!"

When it comes to broken marriages most husbands split the blame - half is his wife's fault, and half is her mother's fault.

Why are there so many in-law jokes?

When you research people, everyone will tell you they are nice people and *baalei tzedakah*. Yet these same people often refuse to chip in for the wedding, or pay more than a minimal amount for a gift for the girl and never invite the young couple for dinner. How many people really have a giving nature? How many people work at being good in-laws?

There are different types of parents-in-law: Some in-laws are great – there when you need them but not too interfering or critical. Other in-laws don't give much, but stay out of their children's lives. Difficult in-laws do not give much in the way of help, friendship or support, yet do interfere. Some in-laws give a lot and expect a lot. Some just enjoy giving and don't need anything in return. Some in-laws don't give anything and demand a lot in return. There are also in-laws who just give a lot of guilt. When you call, they say, "Why haven't you called? We were so worried about you." If they were so worried, why didn't they call you? Do they think you changed your phone number and left no forwarding address?

Ideally parents-in-law should have the same open, honest, giving, and sharing relationship with their child-in-law as they have with their child. Just as parents love their children despite their flaws, they should accept and love their in-law children. Similarly, the way children accept and love their parents, they should accept and love their in-laws. One needs to work at it. Adults who are more experienced in life should be the smart ones, working hard to start the relationship on a good footing. If in-laws are good to their children-in-law, they will see it reciprocated. Everyone prefers to have a good relationship.

Why is the same woman loved by her daughter yet hated by her daughter-in-law?

One woman says, "I have the worst daughter-in-law. She's so lazy. My son has to get up with the kids, make them breakfast and get them off to school. She needs his help with dinner and he has to fix everything around the house." The other woman says, "I have the best son-in-law. He *schleps*. He gets the kids up. He gets them dressed. He gets them off to school. He tells them stories at night. He helps cook and he fixes everything around the house." When your son is working hard you are upset but when your daughter is benefiting, you see it differently.

Some of it involves chemistry. People who plan to be great daughters-in-laws may turn out to be terrible ones and vice versa.

People who think they will be wonderful in-laws turn out to be disappointments and vice versa. Everyone must try to be as good as they can be. It can be tough to make things work smoothly, yet it's rewarding if everyone can be giving and forgiving.

My cousin Neelie has a married daughter. Faigee's mother-in-law constantly calls Neelie to thank her for Faigee, saying how blessed she feels with her son married to such a girl. This mother-in-law does everything for Faigee. No wonder Neelie and Faigee love her. Not only is she giving, she makes Faigee, her daughter-in-law, and Neelie, her daughter- in-law's parents, feel special, appreciated and loved.

First Boy: "I got this bottle of wine for my mother-in-law."
Second boy: "What a great trade!"

WAYS TO GET ENGAGED

When I proposed it was very simple and straightforward. I said, "I want you for my wife." She responded, "What on earth would your wife do with me?"

How often have I heard a boy say, "I'm going to propose as soon as I think of a way."

Here are some ways:

Fill a car with balloons; when the girl opens the door they all fly out.

Order a pizza with "Will you marry me?" written on it in olives or peppers.

Go to a beach at night with wine, glasses and a ring and write a proposal in the sand.

Climb up a fire escape and make a surprise visit. (Of course this has to be prearranged with a family member so the police don't arrest you, the girl doesn't get petrified, and everyone is properly dressed.)

Hire a helicopter. Fly down and swoop the girl in, throwing out candy kisses or balloons.

Hire a horse and buggy and go for a romantic ride through Central Park.

Rent a billboard on a highway, the Long Beach Bridge or Met stadium.

Choose a popular place like The Met, The Empire State Building or The Statue of Liberty and have someone video you asking.

Write a song.

Propose on a roller coaster.

Propose on a picnic.

Skywrite your proposal.

Order dessert and write your feelings on the cake.

Dena was at a restaurant with her friends and called her boyfriend from a phone booth. She was worried about their relationship which seemed to be going nowhere, and she couldn't concentrate on studying for her finals. The boy answered, "Open the door to the phone booth. Now stick out your head. Now yell out to your friends 'Mazel Tov, I'm engaged.'"

Someone put a ring in a cake. Rumor has it, the girl swallowed the ring and had to have her stomach pumped.

Fly to Israel. Goldy was on her way to Israel to pay a surprise visit to her boyfriend. His mother found out about it and asked Goldy to take a package for her son. Then she called her son to tell him Goldy was surprising him. "I sent the ring with Goldy, though she doesn't know it," she added. Goldy arrived in Israel and gave the package to her boy friend. He handed it back to her and asked her to marry him. The surprise was on her.

Asher hired a stretch limo full of balloons and pulled up in front of Stern College to wait for his girlfriend so he could propose to her. A truck drove by and hit the limo. Furious, the limo driver jumped out, causing the balloons to fly up and away. Asher wanted to find his girlfriend, but the limo driver grabbed him, insisting he stay as witness. The police further detained him. By the time Asher got away, the girl had left and he was utterly frustrated because his proposal plan was ruined. He decided to propose the next night, rehiring the limo. This time he succeeded.

Sometimes proposals are memorable without being planned. My husband drove me to a park in Chicago and a cop shined his light in my husband's eyes, while he was making a beautiful speech, demanding to know why we were there. My husband politely said, "Sorry, officer, I was just asking this little lady to be my wife," and showed him the ring. Embarrassed, the officer backed off, saying, "Well, go right ahead... I mean, don't let me interrupt... I mean..." I'm sure he went home to tell everyone what happened. My husband and I had a good laugh since the policeman had been prepared for a drug bust, rather than a proposal. He surely helped make our engagement more memorable.

Jay's parents called Mira's parents saying their children either had to get engaged or stop seeing one another, since they had gone out three times. Jay's parents insisted on a *vort* that night. Her parents convinced Mira to go through with it because she wasn't ready to give him up. During the *vort*, Jay said to Mira, "I guess we'll get married, alright?" And they did!

My cousin Basha dated a boy and continually drilled him with questions. She prepared new lists of questions for each date. After nine weeks of dating he said to her, "Can I ask you one question?" She said, "Okay." And he asked, "Now are you ready to marry me?" She was.

Sometimes a girl is surprised by the proposal, while at other times the couple has already decided they are going to be married and the proposal just seals the deal. Sometimes the couple has the hall, the date, and the gown before the engagement. No matter the style, the proposal has deep significance and should be done with warmth, romance or comedy. Of course, keep your priorities straight. It is not the proposal that is important; it is the person who is proposing.

I have a friend who says her husband is the head of the family. However she is the neck and whichever way the neck moves the head follows.

ENGAGEMENT AND WEDDING

Besides "I love you," what three words does a wife want to hear most? "I'll fix it."

When do you know that this is Mr. or Mrs. Right?

Are you excited this person likes you? Are you glad he's coming for a visit? Are you excited she wants to see you again? Are you waiting for his phone calls? Do you feel empty when you don't hear from him? Are you happy to hear her voice when she picks up the receiver? Are you worried he may not call? Are you nervous she may not consent to the date? If so, the feelings are right. But is this person right for you? Does he or she have what you need? Remember that everyone's needs are different. This person doesn't have to satisfy every need. S/he isn't replacing everyone else in your life, just being added to them. But you do spend a lot of alone time with your spouse, and your new existence has your spouse as a center point.

Does s/he make you feel good about yourself? Not every person is expressive and some are shy or embarrassed to compliment you. But his attitude should give you a sense of "S/he likes me, respects my opinions, and is proud to be with me."

Does she make you feel proud to be with her? Does he make you feel you're lucky to have him? Are you caught up in "What will my friends think" or "Perhaps s/he is heavy but when my friends get to know him they will see what I see in him."

Do the things you love about him or her far outweigh the things that bother you?

Do you feel the two of you can meld together, relate to each other, grow together, accept each other's differences and flaws, positively influence each other, mutually respect each other and head in the same direction? It's a long road with lots of twists and turns. Can you be totally comfortable and open with each other? In an ideal marriage you and your spouse are best friends. You may have separate interests and different opinions, yet you still communicate and connect. There are lots of marriages where the spouses share common goals regarding the support of a family, and raising children, etc. though they never become good friends. That may make a marriage, but it's better to find someone who is your friend. Find someone whom you can confide in, grow with, share with, enjoy with and dream with together.

It is nice to see people transform from their uptight, insecure, unsure attitude prior to their engagement to a confident, happy, comfortable attitude after the engagement. Before the commitment is made, people analyze and dissect every aspect of the person and the relationship. Once the commitment is made, you can enjoy your decision.

I asked one grandmother how well her granddaughter and *chosson* know each other. She answered that they had a better relationship than most. He even asked her to come with him to choose the *benchers*.

Though many couples do not know each other well, they have checked each other out as thoroughly as they can. They have met and determined they are compatible. The engagement period is a time when they can work together and strengthen their relationship. For couples already close, this period is used to enjoy, plan and further grow together.

A long courtship and short engagement may be a good rule. Getting engaged is easy but the engagement period can be tough. It is a good idea for both sets of parents to discuss the wedding and payment of it before an engagement is announced, since this can be a source of disharmony. Working things out without the pressure of the couple already being engaged, is helpful. Discuss the number of people attending and the location of the wedding hall. Who will pay for what? Discuss the *vort* and the *Ofruf*. Discuss supporting or not supporting the kids, their education, their housing, and their future (see chapter "Support"). By compromising and cooperating, parents won't hurt the couple's relationship. Include the couple in the discussions. It's their lives. They must know how they are going to live.

Having a beautiful wedding is not the goal. Working out your future, agreeing about your goals and dreams, negotiating your differences, and deciding policies, etc. is the proper way to start. If people put the amount of effort into a marriage as they do into the wedding, we'd have fewer divorces.

One friend is still paying off the loans he took out for his two daughter's weddings, which he had made years ago. Both his daughters are divorced and he is still paying for the weddings.

Parents must be aware that it is not their wedding, and they should listen with an open mind to their children's desires. On the other hand, kids must know that the parents are paying for the wedding, working on the wedding and have also waited impatiently for this special day. With these attitudes, the young couple and their parents can work together, compromise, and take each other's wishes into consideration.

One can expect uncomfortable conversations about who pays for what, how many guests each side can bring and how many guests the young couple can have. There is no rule except compromise. These decisions are based on how much each side can afford or is willing to pay. It also depends on how many friends, family and obligations each side has. The size of the wedding hall is also a consideration.

Weddings today are enormous because everyone wants all their friends and relatives to share in their *simcha*. The cost and energy that goes into making a wedding is almost prohibitive.

Of course it's more than you can afford. That's the American Way!

Although some people can afford elaborate weddings, the majority find it difficult to cope with the cost of these affairs. According to The Jewish Observer, the cost of marrying off a child will average from $60,000 to $70,000 – a combined figure for both families - and can easily exceed $100,000 (weddings have cost in the millions). This is only for one child. Imagine the burden for those who have six or fourteen children.

Many families feel they must keep up with the Jones's. There are different ideas for limiting the exorbitant expense. These include: eliminating either the *L'chaim* or the *vort*. Magnificent gowns are available for rent from various *Gemachs* (Charities that provide items for a minimal donation). This not only cuts costs, it is also a way of giving *tzedakah*. Limiting the amount of musicians is also cost effective. A single man with great musical equipment usually runs about $850, while the average price for a band is $3,000-$5,000. Renting silk flowers through different organizations is also a terrific idea and helps support the institution. (A centerpiece can range from as little a $15 to the more elaborate $50, going as high as $125 to create your own. These can become part of the rental pool after your affair and help generate income for the organization.) There are now

Gemachs for clothing, flowers, silver and crystal, tablecloths and even uncut cakes. Your *shul* should have a list of these *Gemachs*. The cost of catering also ranges from as little as $38.50 to $125.00 a couple and can be as much as $250 per person. This often does not include extras such as coat check and valet parking. Limiting the pictures to some extent can be helpful in limiting costs. It is essential to capture this precious moment but it is not necessary to capture every move. The wedding seems eventful and momentous, but as life progresses, you barely have time to look at your wedding pictures. You are busy, with G-d's help, taking pictures of your children and eventually your grandchildren.

New *simcha* guidelines are suggested by such organizations as Agudath Israel. Many exact details are still being researched and analyzed to see if they are realistic and beneficial. As it stands now, a ceiling of four hundred invited seated guests is suggested. To accommodate large families, they have suggested a limit of two hundred and fifty guests plus close relatives with the total still remaining under five hundred, excluding children under seventeen. More guests can be invited after the *chupah* or after the meal for a *Simchas Chassan V'kallah* consisting of cakes and fruits or the smorgasbord menu. The smorgasbord is limited to cakes, fruit and four hot dishes, without any carving stations. A bar and Viennese table are discouraged, though wine and liquor can be placed on the tables. No more than five musicians, including the vocalist, is encouraged. Centerpieces should be ordered for the women's tables only, with the total cost not exceeding $1,800. Allowing only chicken for the main dish or permitting meat as well - which some people believe is required for a *seudah* - is still under consideration. Mementos should be something simple like a *bencher*. Gifts between the *chassan* and *kallah* are also limited. The Rabbis designing these rules will not attend weddings that deviate from these guidelines. A symbol, placed on invitations, note that these rules are being followed.

The guidelines may not be perfect for everyone but the idea is admirable; some form of these suggestions should be put into practice. It can help everyone financially as well as improving our value system. The message of not going overboard on a one night affair is valid. Don't spend more than you can afford in order to impress others. Make it a *simcha,* not a competition.

Without doubt the affair will be just as special without the extra expenses. This is not an attempt to hurt florists, photographers, caterers or musicians, but affairs on a more reasonable financial and psychological level must be attempted.

Arrange for different organizations to collect and distribute the left-over food after the smorgasbord. You can ask your caterer to arrange this. You'll feel good about it.

People have reverted to the once popular policy of inviting people only to the smorgasbord and *chupah,* or only to dancing and dessert. People invited only to part of the wedding should not feel slighted. It is difficult to invite everyone. This idea is especially useful for the couple's young friends. They like their friends to be at the wedding, but there are only so many that you can invite to the entire affair. Invite their closest friends to the entire wedding and the rest to share in some part. This idea also works for parent's acquaintances, or people you must invite since they invited you to their affair. They will be happy to reciprocate in the same manner, which works out well for everyone.

People are embarrassed to be the first to cut back. A woman, asked to host a meeting in her home, was told to be the first to change the policy of serving a lot of food; the pressure of providing food was making it hard for the organization to find hosts. The woman agreed with the idea but felt uncomfortable being the first to institute this policy. It might make her look cheap rather than smart.

I admired one boy who sent letters to his friends explaining that although he wanted to invite them for the entire wedding, it would be a financial drain on his future father-in-law, so he was inviting them for the *chupah* and dancing.

Making an expensive wedding is like driving your Rolls Royce to the wedding hall and leaving it there forever.

Although *Rabbanim* and community leaders have addressed this issue, some *simchas* have become more elaborate. Parents, realizing there are better uses for this money, want to cut back, but sometimes the young couple want their dream wedding. And once you have made an elaborate wedding for one child, the others want the same. An overhaul in our way of thinking and in our value system is necessary

Cutting back on the cost of *simchas* and ear-marking those savings as charity is a wonderful idea. An affair with fewer flowers, less musicians, and chicken rather than beef, accompanied by a beautiful note saying the money saved is going to Israel, is admirable.

A wedding is special because of the warmth, *ruach*, joy and the love that pervades the atmosphere.

Doing flip-flops?

In many religious circles the girl's side pays for the hall and caterer while the boy's side pays for "Flops".

1. **F**lowers
2. **L**iquor
3. **O**rchestra
4. **P**hotographer
5. **S**heitel

This rule is not set in stone. This works if both sides are basically equal in financial status.

According to this formula, what each side pays is supposedly equal. The difference in the cost of the wedding payment is made up by the cost of the jewelry the boy's side purchases for the girl.

One of the most difficult tasks in the world is to convince women that even a bargain costs money.

Sometimes, people negotiate the wedding and support before the couple dates. They may consent to the date saying if it works out they can't help with the wedding, or can only pay up a certain amount. Other people make it clear immediately that they do or do not "believe in flops."

One boy's parents said they were paying for their daughter's wedding, so they wanted their son to date girls whose parents agreed to pay for the entire wedding.

The boy buys the girl the engagement ring. Engagement gifts such as a bracelet or pendant are appropriate, and a man's wedding band and pearls for the *kallah* may be given in the *yichud* room. These gifts are optional and vary in price and value depending on what one can afford.

One rabbi said a boy's parents should buy a nice ring for the girl even if they have to go into hock. While that is extreme, everyone should certainly give the best ring they can afford. Give her something she will love to wear.

A woman was wearing a ten-carat diamond ring. All her friends were admiring it when she said, "Yes. It is beautiful. But it comes with the Goldberg Curse."

"What," they all asked, "is the Goldberg Curse?"

"It comes," she answered, "with Mr. Goldberg."

It is widely accepted for the girl's family to buy the boy a watch, a *tallis*, an *atara* (silver collar for the *tallis*), a *tallis* bag, a set of *Shas*, and if he wants, a wedding band.

Some people buy cufflinks for the boy to receive in the *yichud* room. Many times, the couple gives one another meaningful items or fun things in the *yichud* room such as personalized *Tehillim* or roller blades.

Parents can choose these items. Some people like the bride and groom to choose their gifts, and some like to surprise them.

Decisions of which wedding hall, the colors of the wedding party, which band, which photographer, which florist, who walks down the aisle, who sings, what songs are sung, who writes the *ketubah*, etc. should be decided jointly.

Mixed seating versus separate seating, the *mechitzah*, whether to take pictures of the couple before or after the ceremony, who stands under the *chupah*, speeches under the *chupah*, a *mitzvah tantz* (*chassidish* dance at end of a wedding), a *mezinka tantz* (dance when marrying off a last child) and any other family *minhagim* or preference, must also be discussed.

The man leads the woman to the altar at a wedding ceremony – after which his leadership ends.

The boy picks his Rabbi as the *mesader kiddushin* (officiating rabbi). He also picks the witnesses for the ceremony and the *Yichud* room. The bride and groom decide together who will be honored with reciting the seven *brachos* under the *chupah*, reading the *ketubah*, and saying the final seven *brachos* after the meal. These honors are usually given to the most respected rabbis and closest relatives.

Jewish prenuptial papers can also be drawn up by a Rabbi, guaranteeing a "get" if, G-d forbid, the marriage does not work. It is sad to think of this at such a happy, hopeful time of life, but it can save lives later.

The engagement period is rife with tension but can still be an exciting, fun-filled time complete with anticipation and love. Cooperate to make this a wonderful period for everyone involved. This will set a precedent for a smooth, happy marriage.

Only two things are necessary to make a woman happy. First, let her think she's having her way. Second, let her have it.

WEDDING CHECK LIST

A man buys the most expensive scuba diving equipment, a designer mask, the state-of-the-art oxygen tank etc. Then he rents the most expensive luxury yacht, goes out in the middle of the ocean and dives into the water. He goes down twenty feet and is shocked to meet a man wearing only a bathing suit. "I can't believe this," he shouts. "I spend a fortune to buy the most outstanding equipment and you come down here in only a cheap bathing suit." "You moron," cries the other man, "I'm drowning!"

A wedding can be a no frills affair or elaborate. The important element must be love.

Check your community calendar for conflicts when deciding the wedding date. Look at *shul*, school and organizational dinner calendars. Be sure close friends or relatives are not choosing the same date for their affair.

Some people may check that no major sports event is scheduled to air the night of the affair.

Arrange for:

- *L'Chaim*
- *Vort* (*L'Chaim* and *Vort* can be done together)
- *Kallah* and *Chassan* classes
- Engagement party (optional)
- Civil marriage license
- *Ketubah*
- Ring
- Prenuptials (optional)- agreement encouraged by many Rabbis to safeguard against the unfortunate *agunah* situation. (Consult your Rabbi)
- Hall
- Invitations
- Invitation list
- Calligrapher (optional)
- Rabbi
- *Chazzan* and /or singers
- Caterer and menu
- Band (prepare list of songs for the procession and favorite songs to be played during the affair)
- Flowers and bouquets
- *Chupah*
- *Mechitzah*
- Photographer, stills and video (With separate dancing, two video people should be present if possible - one on the men's side and one on the women's)
- Parking

- Coat check
- Place cards (these can be personal ones or provided by the caterer)
- *Kaballas Panim* (the main greeting room where the bride sits)
- *Chassan's Tish* (Groom's welcoming room)
- Program (optional) - It is nice to list the names and relationship of those who are walking down the aisle. This limits the noise level of people inquiring who each person is.
- Letter to guests (optional) - This can be combined with the program.
- *Yarmulkas* (optional)
- *Benchers*
- *Tehillim* (optional) Excerpts are handed out and read silently during the ceremony. These are prayers for the couple, for one's self and for *Klal Yisroel.* They can be borrowed for a nominal contribution to certain charitable organizations
- Pamphlet which explains the ceremony and its traditions (optional) Appropriate for weddings of *baalei teshuvah* or where there are non-religious guests, such as perhaps business associates
- Candy or mints to hand out (optional) This encourages people to suck rather than talk during the ceremony
- Person to inform guests to put their cell phones on silent (optional)
- *Shtik-* includes such items as batons, signs, costumes, umbrellas etc.
- Entertainers (optional) - This can be *Yeshiva* boys who juggle, swallow fire or don costumes or masks. They are not necessarily paid but are often part of the friends or relatives. *Chassidish* weddings often have a *Badchan* (rhymer)

List for kallah and women:
- Gown
- Veil

- Petticoat
- Under garments
- Shoes and stockings
- Hair ornaments
- Makeup (Some brides arrange for a make-up person or a dresser to be at the hall)
- Jewelry
- *Sheitel* (for those who wear it after the *chupah*)
- Pocketbook for checks
- Beauty parlor and or make-up appointments

List for chassan and men:

- Suit or tuxedo
- Shirt
- Tie or bow tie
- Under garments
- Shoes and socks
- Cufflinks (if necessary)
- *Yarmulka*
- *Kittel* (white coat for groom)
- Hat (for those who wear one)
- Black coat (for those who wear one. This custom originates from the fact that weddings in Europe were held outdoors and due to the cold a coat was worn by the groom.)

Items to bring to the wedding:

- Wine cup
- Dish to break (usually supplied by the caterer. Often people save the pieces)
- Glass to break (usually supplied by the caterer. Often people save the pieces)
- Gifts for *Yichud* room
- Gifts for maids of honor (optional)

- List of people and things to pray for under the *chupah* (It is believed the prayers of a bride and groom are the most clearly heard and answered.)
- *Ketubah*
- Civil marriage license
- Rings
- Copy of seating plan
- List of who's doing what: *Eidim* (witnesses) and those receiving *brachos*
- Arrange for someone to hold bride's jewelry

After wedding arrange for:

- Accommodations for wedding night (bring suitcases)
- Transportation from hall to hotel
- *Sheva brachos* (a week of feasting at which one new guest who did not attend the wedding, called *panim chadashos* - a new face must be present)
- *Tallis*
- *Sheitel* or hats for girl to begin wearing
- Change of clothing for after the wedding and the following day
- *Tefillin* for following morning

It is smart to assign someone to be responsible for the *ketubah*, license, gifts and checks. These items have a tendency to get misplaced.

Pay careful attention to even the minor details of the wedding. Mr. Greenbaum made his daughter's wedding in a hall which had never been used for a kosher affair. His Rabbi oversaw the entire transformation of the kitchen, reviewing every detail with the owner. The night of the affair Mr.Greenbaum was informed that the men's bathroom was filled with platters of food. The Rabbi had told the owner to put lots of food in the "men's room" (meaning the *Chassan's Tish* or the groom's gathering room). The owner, though he thought the idea of putting food in the bathroom was silly, decided it must be another Jewish custom.

Why does the bride have to go to the *Kotel* (Western Wall) ten times before her wedding? She has to get used to *"talking to a wall"*.

Why does a boy have to break the glass at his wedding?

Because it's the last time a boy gets to put his foot down.

WEDDING EMOTIONS

Obviously, raising children is not meant to be easy, or it would not begin with something called labor.

Be conscious of everyone else's feelings during this highly emotional period.

A parent hopes and prays to see his or her children married. Yet, many people get depressed during the engagement period. Even when you are thrilled with your child's choice, the experience is overwhelming. Imagine the feeling if you are not so certain of the person your child has chosen.

Plenty of parents are thrilled and excited, and plenty of people are apprehensive and scared. Others feel shocked, as if they are having an out of body experience. They prepare for the wedding but it seems surreal. Still other parents become nervous wrecks, losing or gaining weight, becoming edgy and overly emotional, crying or yelling at the drop of a hat.

Some people say fathers marrying off their daughters are the most anxious; others say mothers marrying off their sons are worse. Many agree that people are less nervous marrying off a daughter than a son, since the girls usually stay close to their mothers no matter whom they marry. Mothers fear they will lose the close relationship with their sons once they are married.

Someone asked me whether I could handle my son's marriage. I answered, "As well as I handled my daughter's wedding." Between my sobs, my husband's, my other children's, my parents' and my daughter's best friend's, one might have thought we were at a funeral, G-d forbid. Our emotions were out of control though we loved and approved of my future son-in-law. We did wonder if our relationship with my daughter as a married woman would be the same, especially since they were moving to Israel. The joy was immense and my gratitude to *Hakadosh Baruch Hu* was immeasurable, but I felt a part of my soul being torn away. I felt that the balance in my family unit was being thrown into disorder. All of my dreams were becoming a reality, yet I didn't know if I could survive the pain of it.

Now seven years and five grandchildren later, with my daughter and her family, as well as my son and his family, living nearby, I can enjoy the fulfillment of my dream. I am immensely blessed.

When my son started dating, we were nervous, apprehensive and cautious once again. Which girl would be good enough? Which girl could fulfill his needs, grow with him, appreciate him, complement him and be a deserving partner? Which girl would joyously join our family, graciously take him into her family, and at the same time work with my son to create their own precious family? Which girl would possess the ability to comfortably build a loving, giving, accepting relationship with my son, his relatives and his friends? Luckily, we were fortunate to be blessed with one such daughter-in-law and now we are beginning the search for six more daughters and sons-in-law.

Each person deals with their child's or sibling's marriage in a different manner. It is important to feel that your child is marrying the right person who will love and cherish him, and not disrupt the relationship you have with him.

The bride and groom should be aware that individuals are concerned and worried about their own relationship with the person. They should be cognizant of those around them, realizing the psychological changes their relatives and friends are experiencing. The couple must grow together while reassuring every one else they will not grow apart from them. It is beneficial for everyone if the new person who is joining the family becomes part of the family, not a part between the family. Of course, this must be done while giving the new couple time and space to continue developing their own relationship.

Life is too long not to do it right.

BROKEN ENGAGEMENTS

There is something magical about the fact that success almost always comes faster to the boy your wife almost married.

Many people are more excited about being engaged than to whom they are engaged. They spend more time planning the wedding than they do planning their lives.

Think long and hard before you get engaged. Once you're engaged, think long and hard about marrying someone if you're not sure. A broken engagement is tough for a while; a bad or broken marriage is much tougher for much longer.

If you are still questioning your decision during the engagement period, don't ignore your instincts. If you need time, postpone the wedding. If you know it's wrong, call it off.

Why does a broken engagement carry such a stigma? One *Rav* says "*Mazel Tov*" on a broken engagement because a major mistake has been avoided. If you have discovered you are making a mistake, it is smart and courageous to end the relationship before it is too late. Is this a cruel thing to do? It causes lots of pain and disappointment for the other person and families involved. However, marrying someone you don't truly love or trust or whom you feel does not love you is doing a disservice to yourself and the other person. The one who calls it off feels dreadful. But in the long run, it is best for both people involved.

What about the person who was committed to the engagement and unfortunately got hurt? Should this person be stigmatized? Should another person refuse to date either person involved in a broken engagement?

If someone suggests you date someone who experienced a broken engagement, discover the issues. It may be important to know why the engagement was broken. Were they both good people but not for each other? Was one unable to make a long- term commitment? Did one of those involved discover something distasteful about the other? Was the couple pressured to get engaged before both were absolutely certain? Often, though not always, it is not one person's fault. The couple either realizes they are incompatible or one of them feels it is not what he wants for a lifetime. A person may not have been right for the person s/he was engaged to, but may be perfect for you.

Can someone who just went through a broken engagement be ready for a new relationship? Can the one who broke the engagement make a sincere commitment? Can the one who got hurt be ready for a new courtship? Both may be very vulnerable. Nevertheless, the person may be right and ready for you. Many people marry girls or boys who were previously and even recently engaged and their marriages work out well.

As in all relationships, judge each person for themselves, look into the circumstances and give everyone a fair chance.

Adam and Eve had a wonderful marriage. Adam couldn't bring up his mother's cooking, and Eve couldn't talk about the man she was supposed to marry!

MARRIAGE

The new bride gushed to her mother, "My husband is very good to me. He gives me everything I ask for." Her mother said, "That only shows you're not asking for enough."

The most difficult years of marriage are those following the wedding.

Daring to discuss the topic of marriage in one chapter is absurd. I will just outline some food for thought.

Kids often think marriage solves all their problems. It only solves the problem of whom you are going to marry! You have someone to build and shape your life with, and a partner with whom to share life's adventures, but now you have the awesome job of building that life and sharing the challenges it brings. You are both new at completely sharing with and answering to a spouse. The two of you must learn to live with one another and for one another. You must learn to run a house, balance a family budget, coordinate your schedules, complete your educations and pursue your learning and careers. You must balance your own needs, the needs of your spouse and still reserve time for your respective families. You must develop common friendships while retaining your old ones. The challenges are exciting and unending. You also begin the greatest challenge of all, building and raising a family.

The things that seemed natural and simple when your parents were doing it, suddenly take on a new form. Even children from large families, who always helped their parents, are initially overwhelmed when the responsibility falls directly on them. It takes time to grow into a couple and into parenthood. You and your spouse must work together, share the responsibilities and communicate your needs, fears and frustrations. Share your learning experiences and your successes. Appreciate each other, encourage each other, and compliment each other. Don't put each other down; rather raise each other's self esteem. Function as a couple. Work together to achieve your dreams.

A smart wife sees through her husband. A good wife sees him through.

Decide what you want from your spouse and then you strive to be that kind of person. Two people who try to please one another make a good marriage. The best people put themselves in the other person's shoes. If each person tries to make the other one happy and satisfy the other person's needs, each one will find that they are happy and fulfilled by the marriage.

A man said that when he and his wife got married, they agreed never to go to bed angry at each other. They haven't slept in seven years.

Be committed to the marriage. Never walk out on each other and never go to bed angry at one another. Discuss your differences, but when issues over which you can argue for hours arise, stop and tell each other that you love one another; somehow you really will find a compromise.

A comprehensive police study showed that no wife has ever shot her husband while he was doing the dishes.

I told a married boy that my daughter does not want to mold a husband. He said, "She will." Every girl molds and teaches her husband. (Married men often wonder how they ever got dressed without their wives telling them what was appropriate to wear). Truthfully, each person molds the other one while s/he is simultaneously being molded, and life molds the two of you.

"Is your husband hard to please?"
"I don't know I never tried!"

Try not to fight, but if things do bother you, pick your fights. Concentrate on what is important to you. You are the one who has to live with your spouse. It can be frustrating if something about your husband or wife bothers someone else, and possibly that should be addressed. But if it doesn't bother you, don't let it hurt your marriage. Don't let someone else's hang-ups become your hang-ups. We each have enough hang-ups and concerns of our own!

Rabbi Paysach Krohn says a couple can have their differences but they need to "agree to disagree", dealing respectfully with their differences.

Marriage classes that deal with relationships and meeting one another's needs, as well as the religious laws of sexual conduct, should be taken prior to the marriage. Couples experiencing difficult adjustments in their marriage should be encouraged to seek marital counseling right away.

"There's nothing more important than approaching your own doorstep and knowing that someone on the other side is listening for the sound of your footsteps." *(Ronald Reagan)*

Two Texas political candidates were having a heated debate. One shouted, "What about the powerful interests that control you?"
The other screamed back, "You leave my wife out of this."

As the man, you get to apologize. What does the woman get to do? She gets to forgive you. My sister Esti once suggested that husbands call home everyday and spontaneously say "I'm sorry" to their wives, as the best way to keep a marriage strong. "Don't worry," Esti added, "the wife will always think of a reason why her husband is sorry."

A man took his wife to a psychiatrist and said, "What's-her-name here complains that I don't give her enough attention!"

There is a *Yeshiva* rule that a boy who is learning must go home daily for lunch during the first year of marriage, to spend time with his new wife. Furthermore, he cannot learn at night without his wife's permission. This rule was instituted because the *Yeshivas* are trying to foster good marriages. Spend a lot of time together during your first years of marriage. Make your spouse a priority and discuss your schedules. Life only gets more complex.

Marriage is a two way street, which accounts for all the head-on collisions!

Work together, sharing the chores and responsibilities. A woman came to Rav Gifter complaining that her husband refused to help her take out the trash because it was beneath him. The following morning the *Rav* showed up at the woman's home to take out her garbage. Rav Gifter wanted to show the husband that if it was not beneath a great *Rav*'s dignity to help with the garbage, it certainly was not beneath the husband's dignity to help with the garbage.

Each spouse must help the other achieve personal as well as common goals. A supportive wife will tell her husband, "I'll work and clean up and take care of the kids so you can learn." Nevertheless when she is overwhelmed because the baby is crying, she may say to her husband, "Wait. Where are you going?" She needs him. A couple must find balance. Prioritize your goals, but more importantly, make each other's needs your priority.

Shimon told his *Rebbe* he was late to *Yeshiva* because on his way he saw a woman struggling with two little infants, getting them down the stairs, *schlepping* the carriage and putting them on the bus. He decided to help this woman put her kids on the bus. After all, they were his kids too! Studying and learning teaches one to become a better, more caring, more feeling person and to grow in one's *midos*. Find someone who understands the value of being a good person, a good spouse and a good parent! Be a husband or wife with these same values!

A young woman confided that it could take up to a year of marriage to fall in love with your spouse. This may be true, but it is important to marry someone whom you think you love, or at least are certain you can grow to love. By identifying qualities you admire in one another and working together towards your mutual goals, your relationship and love will flourish.

Grow together, age together, mature together. Enjoy one another. Enjoy life.

Harry was stunned to come home from work one evening and find his wife stuffing all her belongings into a suitcase. "What on earth are you doing?" he cried.

"I can't stand it any more!" she shrieked. "Thirty-two years we've been married, and all we do is bicker and quarrel and ignore each other. I'm leaving!"

Stunned, Harry watched his wife close the suitcase, lug it down the stairs and proceed to walk out of the house...out of his life.

Suddenly, he was galvanized into action. Running into the bedroom and grabbing a second suitcase, he yelled back at his wife, "Sylvia, you're right, you're absolutely right and I can't bear it either. Wait a minute, I'll go with you."

DIVORCE

Woman to marriage counselor: "The only thing my husband and I have in common is that we were married on the same day."

The psychiatrist had a tremor in his voice as he told Mr. Cooper, "I regret that I have to tell you this - your wife's mind is gone." Mr. Cooper said, "I'm not surprised. She's been giving me a piece of it every day for twenty years."

A woman went to an attorney and said, "I want to divorce my husband."

The lawyer asked, "Do you have any grounds?"

"About 10 acres," the woman said.

Lawyer: "Do you have a grudge?"

Woman: "No, just a carport."

Lawyer: "Does your husband beat you up?"

Woman: "No, I get up about an hour before he does every morning."

Lawyer: "Why do you want a divorce?"

Woman: "We just can't seem to communicate."

"I don't think I'll get married again. I'll just find a woman I don't like and buy her a house." *(Lewis Grizzard)*

Unfortunately, there are many divorces today. People don't want to work at their marriages. Spouses must communicate their needs to each other, satisfying the needs of the other, without losing sight of their own needs. Compromise, adjust, and be more understanding, accepting, giving and loving. Marriage takes work. Marrying the person right for you is the first step. Appreciating your spouse over time, with the ever changing dynamics of the relationship and the challenges life presents us, calls for effort and adjustments. Then you will have a successful and lasting marriage.

Sometimes you make the right decision. Sometimes you have to make the decision right.

You can walk away from a date; marriage is not like that! Today people often rush to get divorced. Someone who organizes events for singles told me couples contemplating divorce should come to a single's weekend. Of course someone who is truly unhappy should not remain in a bad marriage. Being married and miserable is not normal. Marriage should be a happy and fulfilling experience.

There are many books and tapes as well as many great marriage counselors and Rebbeim who are equipped to help couples in this area. Couples suffering from problems or differences should not be embarrassed to turn to someone for help. Many young couples consult Rabbis and marriage specialists who help them work through their differences to structure a good marriage.

There would be a lot more happy marriages if husbands tried to understand their wives and wives tried to understand football.

THE HAPPY ENDING

One day the Israeli soldier at the checkpoint on the military highway addressed the Arab riding along on his donkey, his aged wife trudging before him. "I've been watching you go by every morning for months," the guard commented, "and you always ride and your wife is always on foot. Why?"

"Wife no have donkey," replied the Arab with a shrug.

"I see. But why does she walk in front of you? Is that the custom of your people?"

The Arab shook his head. "Land mines," he explained.

The most important elements of a good relationship are kindness and respect. The search for the right person can be difficult but the reward is a lifetime of giving and receiving love, of sharing and growing together, of learning from one another and leaning on each other, of laughing and crying together and, with G-d's help, growing old together as you raise a beautiful and *Torahdik* family.

True love doesn't consist of holding hands - it consists of holding hearts.

Love is a little word; people make it big.

I pray that every one of you finds true and lasting love.

GLOSSARY

Aliyah	Permanent residence in Israel
Aveilus	A year of mourning after a relative's death
Baal Chessed	Doer of good deeds
Baal Aliyah	One who is growing in Judaism
Baal Teshuva	Returnee to religious Judaism
Baalei Tzedakah	Charitable people
Bas Ploni L'Ploni	Daughter of so-and-so to so-and-so
Bashert	Destined partner
Bekovedik	Respectful
Bitachon	Trust in G-d
Blatt of Gemara	Page of the Talmud
Chachmas Lev	Smart, understanding heart
Chassan	Groom
Chassan Tish	Groom's party
Chassidish	Hasidic; Related to Hasidism
Chavrusa/s	Learning partner/s
Chazal	Acronym for "our Sages of blessed memory"; commentary
Chessed	Good deed
Chinuch	Teaching
Chovos Halevovos	"Duties of The Heart" – a Jewish ethical book
Chupah	Wedding ceremony or bridal canopy
Daven	Pray
Divrei Torah	Words of Torah
Emunah	Faith in G-d
Eretz Yisroel	Israel
Farher	Test
Frum	Observant
Gelt	Money
Get	Orthodox divorce
Glacha	Perfect, smooth
Heimish	Homey; reference to a certain type of Jewish personality
Hakadosh Baruch Hu	G-d
Hakoras Hatov	Appreciation

Halachik/Halachically	According to Torah law
Hashem	G-d
Hashgachos	Kashrus certification
Hashkafah	Religious outlook
Hatzalah	Ambulance service
Heter/Heteirim	Permission(s) to bypass the laws
Hishtadlus	Effort
Kaheref Ayin	In a blink of an eye
Kal Vachomer	How much more so
Kallah	Bride
Kashrus	Kosher
Ketubah	Marriage certificate
Kiddush Levanah	Blessing on the new moon
Kedushah	Holiness
Kiruv	Bringing others close to religion
Kishkas	Guts
Klaf	Parchment containing a prayer, inside a mezuzah
Kohen	Descendant of priests
Kollel	School for married full time learners
Kovaya Itim	Establish set time for Torah study
Kriyas Yam Suf	Splitting of the Red Sea
Kumzitz	Sing along
L'Chaim	Toast
Lashon Hara	Slander
Lekaf Zechus	Giving one the benefit of the doubt
Lev	Heart
Lo Sa'amod al Dam Rei'echa	Do not stand by while your brother's blood is spilled
Maariv	Evening prayers
Mechutanim	In-laws
Makom	Place
Mekubal	Kabbalistic Rabbi
Mashgiach	Overseer
Mazel	Luck
Mazel Tov	Congratulations
Mechitzah	Partition between men and women
Mezinka	Dance for parents marrying off their last child

Mentch	Decent human being
Mentch Tracht un Gut Lacht	"Man plans and G-d laughs"
Mesiras Nefesh	Sacrificing for others
Midah/Midos or Midot	Character trait/s
Midakdek	Exacting
Midrash	Story of Talmudic or Midrashic origin
Midvar Sheker Tirchok	Distance yourself from lies
Min Hashamayim	Heavenly ordained
Minhagim	Traditions
Mesader Kiddushin	Officiating Rabbi at a wedding
Mitzvah Tantz	Chassidic wedding dance
Mitzvah/Mitzvos	Good deed/s
Mizaveg Zivugim	Makes matches
Moshiach	Messiah
Motzei Shem Ra	Give a bad name
Nachas	Pride
Neshamos	Souls
Nisayon/Nisyonos	Test/s
Nogayah	Relevant
Ofruf	Groom is called to the Torah prior to his wedding
Olam Habah	World to Come
Panim Chadashos	Person attending the Sheva Brachos who was not at the wedding
Parnassa	Means of earning a living
Parshah	Chapter/Topic
Pirkei Avot	Ethics of the Fathers
Poseik	One who interprets the laws
Rabbeim/Rabbanim	Rabbis/Teachers
Rav	Rabbi
Rebbetzin	Rabbi's wife
Rebbi/Rebbeim	Rabbi/s
Rhed	Lit. "speak" - Arrange
Rosh/ei Yeshiva	Head/s of the Yeshiva
Schlep	Drag
Sefer/Seforim	Book/s
Shabbos	Saturday/Sabbath

Shabbos Nachamu	Saturday following the Ninth of Av
Shabbaton	Weekend
Shadchan	Matchmaker
Shadchanus	Having to do with being an intermediary or shadchan
Shas	The Talmud
Shayach	Relevant
Sheitel	Wig
Sheva Brachos	Seven Blessings/Seven days of parties following the wedding
Shidduch/im	Match/es
Shiur/im	Class/es
Shir Hashirim	Song of Songs
Shivah	Seven days after a relatives death when one receives visitors
Shmiras Halashon	Guarding your speech
Shtusim	Mundane things/Stupidities
Shul	Synagogue
Simchos/Simchas	Happy occasions
Siyatah D'shmayah	Divine Intervention
Tachlis	Serious marriage intentions
Tallis/Talleisim	Prayer shawl/s
Talmidei Chachamim	Learned students
Talmid/im	Student/s
Tehillim	Psalms
Torah U'Madda	Learning and working
Torahdik	Follows the Torah ways
Tzedakah	Charity
Vort	Engagement party
Yarmulka	Skullcap
Yerushah	Inheritance
Yeshiva	School of religious studies
Yeshivish	Yeshivah educated/Right wing
Yichud Room	Private room for bride and groom following the ceremony
Yichus	Heritage/Ancestry
Yomim Tovim	Holidays
Zivug	Match
Z'man	Time/Semester

Notes